SAGE was founded in 1965 by Sara Miller McCune to support the dissemination of usable knowledge by publishing innovative and high-quality research and teaching content. Today, we publish over 900 journals, including those of more than 400 learned societies, more than 800 new books per year, and a growing range of library products including archives, data, case studies, reports, and video. SAGE remains majority-owned by our founder, and after Sara's lifetime will become owned by a charitable trust that secures our continued independence.

Los Angeles | London | New Delhi | Singapore | Washington DC | Melbourne

Advance Praise

At last we have a book that discusses the sales function honestly and introspectively. Written very engagingly, it should form a part of orientation programmes for newcomers to the profession and for students of sales management.

Rama Bijapurkar
Author of *A Never-Before World:*
Tracking the Evolution of Consumer India

Roshan Joseph has a unique style of presenting great concepts and ideas in an uncomplicated and practical manner. *Salespeople Don't Lie* is an easy-read from start to finish and it will change the negative perception about the generic image of a salesperson, using real-life examples. It helps us to recognize the dignity and intricacies of a sales professional and the art of selling, in the right perspective. A must-read for all who like sales!

K.G. Ramani
Head of Sales, Muscat Pharmacy, Oman

Roshan has been there and done that. The authenticity and reality comes alive.

This book can be read at two levels. Firstly a serious analysis of sales processes and best practices. But it can also be read as a fun fact-filled novel of the life of the Indian salesperson. The rooming and boarding in small town India, the wholesale *mandis* in the metro towns, they all come alive and real. A great read.

Kurush Grant
Former Director, ITC

Move over from ad hoc selling to professional selling and create real value for your company! *Salespeople Don't Lie* is a gem of a book from a true practitioner with real-life sales experience of over four decades. It lucidly weaves through innumerable sales situations with deep insight of what works and what is false. A must-read for any sales professional interested in genuinely furthering his sales career.

Sanjeev Vohra
Consultant, Brand Architect

Margin and market share desperation and lack of discipline and systems in sales have made sales processes an act of compromise. With a rich tapestry of relevant and relatable examples, Roshan showcases how sales is more than just selling and makes you intro-spect about how you are positioning yourself and your business to customers and create a sustainable sales system.

Dr Harsha Guduru
Head—Operations, Quality and Training,
One Life Home Healthcare

I have spent most of my working life in sales of one kind or another, the last 30 with the Coca-Cola Company in sales in countries from the UK, Europe, the Middle East and the Far East. This book is well and skilfully written, and I could easily relate to the contents. The book should, in my view, help all salespeople think about how they may improve their results if they go about their business as Mr Joseph suggests.

Ben J.H. Knight
Sales Consultant, Former VP Sales,
Coca-Cola Company, Japan

Roshan Joseph, who spent most of his professional career in sales and marketing, and now as a life coach for thousands of young or old salespeople, demystifies the common belief that 'selling' is another word for 'lying'. Unbelievable as it may seem, the need for honesty integrates most effectively with the contemporary business environment. A must-read for today's sales leadership.

Suvamoy Saha
Director, Eveready Industries India Ltd, Kolkata

Roshan is not only one of those doyens of sales and marketing professionals who have seen and done it all, but he is also a great storyteller—the best way to drive home the truth to salespeople who are basically simple people at heart. He does that extremely well in these pages from the perspective of a professional who has seen the world of selling transform over the decades.

Sandip Ranjan Ghose
Executive President (Sales, Marketing and Logistics),
Birla Corporation Ltd

A thoroughly enjoyable read! Roshan has successfully charted the course to becoming an effective and truthful salesperson. The book is dotted with real-life examples, which give the reader a perspective on practical on-ground situations from various industries. It is heartening to note that salespeople can build businesses resting on skills acquired from this book. A must-read for both entry-level and middle management.

Saugata Mitra
Whole Time Director,
Mother Dairy Fruit & Vegetable Pvt. Ltd

SALES
PEOPLE
~~DON'T~~
LIE

SALES PEOPLE DON'T LIE

ROSHAN L. JOSEPH

Los Angeles | London | New Delhi
Singapore | Washington DC | Melbourne

First published in 2018 by

SAGE Publications India Pvt Ltd
B1/I-1 Mohan Cooperative Industrial Area
Mathura Road, New Delhi 110 044, India
www.sagepub.in

SAGE Publications Inc
2455 Teller Road
Thousand Oaks, California 91320, USA

SAGE Publications Ltd
1 Oliver's Yard, 55 City Road
London EC1Y 1SP, United Kingdom

SAGE Publications Asia-Pacific Pte Ltd
3 Church Street
#10-04 Samsung Hub
Singapore 049483

Published by Vivek Mehra for SAGE Publications India Pvt Ltd, typeset in 12/15 Perpetua by Fidus Design Pvt. Ltd., Chandigarh and printed at Saurabh Printers Pvt Ltd, Greater Noida.

Library of Congress Cataloging-in-Publication Data
Name: Joseph, Roshan L., author.
Title: Salespeople Don't lie / Roshan L. Joseph.
Description: New Delhi, India; Thousand Oaks, California: SAGE Publications India, 2018.
Identifiers: LCCN 2018009404 (print) | LCCN 2018010953 (ebook) | ISBN 9789352807130 (E pub 2.0) |
    ISBN 9789352807123 (pbk) | ISBN 9789352807147 (web)
Subjects: LCSH: Selling. | Sales management.
Classification: LCC HF5438.25 (ebook) | LCC HF5438.25 J67 2018 (print) | DDC 658.85—dc23
LC record available at https://lccn.loc.gov/2018009404

ISBN: 978-93-528-0712-3 (PB)

SAGE Team: Manisha Mathews, Apoorva Mathur, Syeda Aina Rahat Ali and Ritu Chopra
Illustrations Courtesy: Ajoy Joseph

To my wife Joanne, who is my anchor,
my compass and my refuge from the challenges
of each day. Thank you for being you!

Thank you for choosing a SAGE product!
If you have any comment, observation or feedback,
I would like to personally hear from you.

Please write to me at **contactceo@sagepub.in**

Vivek Mehra, Managing Director and CEO, SAGE India.

Bulk Sales

SAGE India offers special discounts
for purchase of books in bulk.
We also make available special imprints
and excerpts from our books on demand.

For orders and enquiries, write to us at

Marketing Department
SAGE Publications India Pvt Ltd
B1/I-1, Mohan Cooperative Industrial Area
Mathura Road, Post Bag 7
New Delhi 110044, India

E-mail us at **marketing@sagepub.in**

Get to know more about SAGE

Be invited to SAGE events, get on our mailing list.
Write today to **marketing@sagepub.in**

This book is also available as an e-book.

Contents

CONTENTS

Foreword

The world of business that my twin daughters have entered today is almost unrecognizable from the one I knew at their age. My generation grew up in relatively placid water and those were the days, when selling was essentially an art practised by a salesperson to forge relationships with customers and communicate how his product met an unmet need of consumers and was better than his competitors. A few corporations like Unilever who believed in 'doing well by doing good' were weaving a purpose into this art.

Unilever has stood the test of time because it believes in 'selling with purpose'. In the 1890s, William Hesketh Lever, founder of Lever Brothers, wrote down his ideas for Sunlight soap—his revolutionary new product that helped popularize cleanliness and hygiene in Victorian England. It was 'to make cleanliness commonplace; to lessen work for women; to foster health and contribute to personal attractiveness, that life may be more enjoyable and rewarding for the people who use our products'.

In the 25 years that I have spent in Unilever, many of them leading businesses in South Asia, Southeast Asia, Middle East and North Africa, I have learnt the importance of integrity and purpose in selling. My friend Roshan L. Joseph drives this very point home in his inimitable and effective style through this book. He has ably expounded the critical role played by the seemingly less important salesperson in an organization. I have known Roshan for nearly three decades. With years of wide and intense experience in sales, marketing, human resources and general management, Roshan provides invaluable insights into selling and the life of a salesperson, consolidating his learnings and the deep passion he has for training and development.

What makes *Salespeople ~~Don't~~ Lie* stand out are the real-life examples that Roshan entwines into his anecdotal style of narrating experiences in a manner that a reader can relate to it. With advent of big data and analytics and the increasing use of artificial intelligence, selling will become more of a science than an art. However, in business, as in life, it is not about 'either or'. As I frequently tell my colleagues, a good salesperson will always have that human touch which will be reflected in the way they build and nurture relationships with their customers. The key to success for an individual as well as an organization is to 'reinvent' themselves, and Roshan has brilliantly illustrated this to amplify how a salesperson can turn into a hero and the role an organization can play in facilitating this journey.

I am delighted to recommend this book and honoured to be asked to contribute a foreword. I believe that every aspiring business leader should spend some time in the sales function. It is in 'sales' where the rubber hits the road and this is where I understood the realities and intricacies of business. I have always remained a salesman—If I am not selling soaps and soups, I am selling ideas and strategies. Whatever selling journey you happen to be in, this book will provide you an interesting perspective.

Sanjiv Mehta
Chief Executive Officer and Managing Director,
Hindustan Unilever Limited

Preface

In writing this book, there has been only one purpose—to focus on the different aspects of a salesperson's life that need to change with a changing world. A career in sales is magnificent and is increasingly drawing youngsters of great potential and talent. There was a time, not long ago, when only those who could not get a job elsewhere applied for a sales job. Not today. Yet there is so little expected from them.

Salespeople lie. No one is surprised to hear this statement. It is a sweeping statement and does not intend to mean that all salespeople lie, all the time. However, it is hard to say with a straight face that salespeople don't lie. Many believe that it is a necessary talent of great salespeople.

This much maligned band of brothers (previously, there were few or no saleswomen, unlike today) are the happiest company one could spend an evening with. These are people of spirit and a view on life that is both cynical and sweet. People who can do audacious things and yet be ready to give all for a friend, especially for the one in need.

I recall the first day I stepped into a sales branch at Brabourne Road, Calcutta (now Kolkata). It was a crummy, disorganized office, where everyone seemed to be moving around scattered tables, piled high with documents. At the end of an uneventful first day, a visiting sales officer, MK, invited me to the Great Eastern Hotel, one of Calcutta's heritage buildings.

Pleased to be so welcomed, I joined MK, who piously produced a bottle of Old Monk rum. Not accustomed to drinking, I politely declined the offer. MK exclaimed that it was impossible to sell in India if one did not drink to get drunk. He prophesied that in a year's time, I would be a great 'drunkard'; otherwise, he would change his name. Neither of those happened.

Across the world, markets give testimony to the stamina and drive of the salespeople tribe. They brave the inclement weather, with rugged determination, travel for days on end, eat food when available and stay in special 'sales' hotels where salespeople from all companies gather. They have one eye on their target and the other on where to find a sucker.

In the Wild West, there were gunslingers, who looked out for the next challenge. It is no different in sales—get a customer before he gets you. The sale is thrust on every resistant customer.

Charming though this may seem, underlying all the mayhem is a real problem. The practice of sales is getting more carnal by the year. Irresponsible selling has had its toll on products, profits, markets and trade. Like a Greek tragedy, the stories on the sales hill are also increasingly ending with dire consequences.

This is the age of everything connected. Privacy and secrets are fodder for a growing and numb audience. Everything can be traced back. Can we hope to still carry on the way we did? All bluster and no substance? All lies and alternate truths? The time is now to promote a 'Swachh Sales' movement. Clean up our act and be accepted into the ranks of the professionals.

This book, written with great affection and hope, is offered to encourage salespeople to be a vital part of, what can so easily be, a worthy and trusted profession. One that makes a mark by adding wealth for customers, by better understanding their needs and by offering solutions that make them more successful. In doing so, contributing to society in a unique way, the professional salesperson will be the one who has no need to lie.

I would like to acknowledge Ajoy Joseph for the great illustrations. He has great talent and a wicked sense of humour. The brilliant illustrations in the book are a testimony to that.

The anecdotes here are those that really happened. I have tried to change names to protect individuals who were part of the story because while the lesson is important, naming the person is not.

1
How Did Salespeople Come To Be?

If one were to be inspired by the stories of salespeople who told lies, nothing is more ominous than the one in the Bible. The first salesperson, according to the Good Book, was none other than the wily serpent, an avatar of Satan. It is said that the first apple to be sold was to Eve, based on a big lie.

It appears that the serpent, while trying to tempt Eve, ran up against the conventional wisdom of Eden that one was not to eat of the fruit, today called the apple. The serpent, however, had a ready 'alternate fact' to push his sale. He claimed that the prohibition was merely to stop man from being as powerful and divine as the Lord. Oh, what a lie it turned out to be! Eve bit into the apple and felt only guilt, not the slightest turbopower charge. Adam and Eve were summarily deported from Eden as illegal aliens.

I have a rather more romantic view of how salespeople came to be.

I imagine a little village baker, who first cracked the puzzle of what one could do with the new grain found growing near the village. Some called it wheat, others thought it poison. Otto saw potential in this wonder grain, powdering the wheat and mixing it with various condiments. He baked it in a makeshift oven and made the first cake. It was an instant hit. He would hardly finish baking when the line of eager first movers grabbed every cake he could produce.

He did not need a salesman.

Seeing the lines form from early in the morning, Otto's wife Nina came up with a bold suggestion of a second oven. His sister Emma thought that he could run a night shift and produce more cakes. Now the lines were not as long as they had known before. In fact, there was even an odd day when there would be cakes left over from the previous day. This bothered Otto as Nina had already placed an order for third oven. There was no online shipping then, yet it could be delivered any day soon.

Otto wondered if his cocky nephew Hans could be encouraged to get more customers for his famous cakes.

Hans was probably the first salesman ever to be hired.

Hans turned out to be just what Otto needed. Hans realized that to get more customers for the cake, he had to increase the availability of the wonder cakes far beyond the limits of their modest village. Hans set up an ingenious system of home delivery to all neighbouring villages. Nina ordered three more ovens and a three-shift, around the clock, production.

Whatever the genesis of the salesperson, the world today has too many salespeople, if the growth of e-commerce is to be considered. More alarming is the way the touch of the serpent has made Hans seem a very naughty boy.

That is putting it mildly.

Sales has become a vocation that is fraught with lies, white lies and statistics. This has made salespeople a subject of scrutiny. Can they be trusted? Do salespeople sell lies or lie to sell?

Or both?

2

The Door-to-door Salesperson

One thing is clear, you need the salesperson only if you have excess stock, after the current demand has been met. It was the Industrial Revolution that really gave an impetus to the growth of the ubiquitous salesperson. Until the advent of factories, the pressure was on making more. Demand was assured. People fought to be the first to buy before it ran out.

Nothing here indicates that the new trend in people carrying products for sale would soon be the start of the modern day, lying salesperson. The first recognized sighting of the salesman was noted along the railroad building boom in America. These travelling salesmen were called 'snake oil' salesmen. It is purely coincidental that the first ever sales act recorded was by a suspicious sales serpent selling the magical powers of an apple.

The back-breaking job of building the mighty railroads had many railroad workers groaning by sunset as their aching muscles screamed for a soothing balm. An oil mixed with a slight proportion of rattle snake venom provided the numbing effect on sore muscles. Or so, they claimed. Soon snake oil with a little help from the salesman's fertile imagination became a multipurpose elixir that could heal without any license.

Competition does many things to an industry and the snake oil success soon had everyone searching for the original recipe, only to discover that it was a simple, well-intentioned hoax. Snake oil sales were soon considered fake and literally hounded out of the market. The shame name remained to identify the type of salesman who was not to be trusted.

The Industrial Revolution produced textiles and clothing in quantities that producers found difficult to dispose. While the mills of Manchester worked overtime to wondrous rhythm of the huge factories, trouble was brewing in paradise. More salespeople were hired as people no longer felt that any product was in short supply. The age of mechanics brought about another type of salesperson: the door-to-door vacuum seller.

The saying 'a foot in the door' originated from this rather 'un-ingenious' selling technique. This was in the early 1930s and 1940s when housewives were not as security conscious and readily opened the door to any salesperson who rang the bell. The moment the door was opened, the sales whiz put his foot on the threshold to avoid the door being slammed on him. With this advantage, he was ready to use all guilt techniques to shame the poor housewife to buying the amazing dust buster.

Appliances were a rarity in those days, and the housewife was very amenable to accepting the benefits of the marvellous machine that could suck dust out of a spotlessly clean sofa. Not being in a position to know better, the salesperson found stretching the truth a very catching habit. It is said that the more times an untruth is repeated, the more it acquires all the respectability of a country parson's Sunday homily.

Historically, 'commercial travellers' in Britain were known to have 'the gift of the gab' and to 'spin a yarn' about their goods. This does not imply that they told lies but put their merchandise in the best possible light to their customers. This was an accepted 'method of operation' and understood and accepted by customers and sales-people alike. Such 'commercial travellers' built up a high degree of trust between themselves and their customers, who they called on regularly, and were well known in the commercial community.

The days of the 'commercial travellers' are now almost over with shops, the telephone, television and computers being the current forms of marketing good and services.

Nevertheless, the question of the 'truth' still applies, probably even more so today. Goods and services are still sold by how they are advertised, the personality of sales staff and the knowledge they can impart honestly to their customers.

Here is when the allure of the fast talking salesman became legendary. Any tot that spoke a lot was designated as a future salesperson. If you spoke a lie fast enough, it could slip past the customer. In time it got so good that it also slipped past the salesperson who really had a tough time disentangling the truth from fiction.

There was no way for the customer to check facts. Google was yet to be. So to every question that she asked, there was an ever entertaining answer and assurance. Salespeople were discovering the power of a lie so easy and so helpful in making a sale. There was really no need to check the facts. You just made them up.

3

The Used Car Salesperson

With the advent of the door-door-salesperson, the growth of the automotive industry and Henry Ford's assembly line production saw cars fly off Detroit's manufacturing facilities, faster than the dealers across the USA could move them off their showrooms. If the railroads spawned the snake oil salespeople, the cars did it for the used car sales wizards.

In a 2002 Gallup poll of the least honest professions, car salespeople and politicians came up as the least trusted. Very few eyebrows are raised at this finding. Consider the experience that awaits the unwitting consumer who steps into a car showroom.

Carol Unity Adams, who has spent years in selling and is now based in London, adds 'One group of sales staff that have continually had a bad reputation in Britain for "spinning a yarn" are car sales staff, particularly second hand car salesmen'. New research found that on over half of used cars sold, money had to be spent by buyers to ensure they were roadworthy. Clearly, the well-known Latin phrase 'caveat emptor' (let the buyer beware) is neither well known enough nor practised properly in the sale of second-hand cars in Britain today!

In fact, only about one-fifth of British folk (18 per cent) trust car salesmen.

Mark Rogers, managing director of 'Sell Car' said: 'From our research it is apparent that there are some people willing to lie about faults with their vehicles in order to sell them. This means that potential buyers are frequently being conned and having to spend additional money on their cars'. He continues: 'When buying or selling your car it is important to consult a trustworthy and fully qualified expert within the car industry to receive an accurate assessment and a fair estimate of price for it'.

'Many times, customers are not as experienced as the salespeople,' says Dr Ekman in his book *Telling Lies*. 'For example, in my lifetime,' he says, 'I have purchased only seven cars. This puts me at a great disadvantage when I talk to salespeople who may sell seven cars a week. Salespeople are more experienced at being convincing and most buyers can't tell if the salesperson is truthful to them'.

Very often, car dealers advertise a very low-priced car. This is just to get the walk-ins. Once there, the consumer is told that every piece was sold out; however, there are a few models on which there are daring discounts. Of course, the prices are much higher than the advertised models.

Once you have stepped into the showroom, car salespeople try to stop you from leaving, even using ploys like blocking the exit with other cars, or if you are trading in your current car, not getting back on time from the appraiser's mandatory test drive.

The world of car selling is a very tough one, and it is interesting to read about Joe Girard, who holds the Guinness record for selling the most number of cars for 12 straight years of his career. No one has ever beaten that record.

It is interesting to know that Joe started selling cars because he had no money to even put food on the table for his family. He had a friend who was in a car dealership. He asked if he could try and sell to even a single customer. It was closing time and a cold January month. Suddenly, a customer came rushing in. He was employed by the Coca-Cola Company. Joe managed to sell him a car. He was stunned with how powerful he felt on closing the sale. He did not really know what he did to make it happen. He was certain he wanted to do it again.

Even though the deal was done, Joe was not able to get his commission the same evening. However, based on the sale, he borrowed $10 to walk into a grocery store and carry home dinner for all.

Therein is the power of selling. Joe realized that he had a manner that customers trusted. They would come to him and ask for him by name. He went on to be an icon with the label 'The Greatest Salesman in the World'.

Yet for every Joe Girard, there are thousands who sell deceptively and get labelled as huckster, charlatan, conman, sleazebag and such.

On every call, salespeople have a choice to do what's right or what's easy and expedient. To do what's right is a question of moral judgement.

In 1785, Thomas Jefferson wrote a letter to Peter Carr, sharing his thoughts on the subject: 'Whenever you are to do a thing, though it can never be known but to yourself, ask yourself how you would act were all the world looking at you, and act accordingly'.

With Internet selling, there is a possibility of bringing this whole industry some greater transparency. However, the tonal quality of the digital media reeks of the sleaze when relationship building is founded on manipulation and not a true concern for meeting the needs of the customer. Websites are designed to take the customer from a hello to a closing deal handshake in the course of few web pages.

Jeff Bezos said it right:

> Amazon helps people make the right decision.
> Not selling, but helping people buy better.

4

Sell Like Hell

In every town, there are specific hotels where the travelling sales-person spends the night. Often, they meet other salespeople, who they have never worked with. Sometimes it is late into the night when they recount their tales of valour. These sessions are rollicking affairs and do much to remove the stress of the hard day they have toiled in the market.

Here one gets to meet all types of salespeople and one can better understand how the work can get so tedious and stressful. As the stories are told, one can find a particular theme which is responsible for much of the mirth that fills the evening. It is generally about how a hapless customer was taken advantage of. In these evening sessions, one realizes that the image of the customer is one of the adversary rather than the partner.

There is a researched finding from Carew International, USA, one of leading sales research and development companies in the USA, that out of 10 salespeople, only about 3 ever think of their customer's benefit, the other 7 are only interested in meeting their quotas, come what may. What makes selling such a toxic pro-fession? Why is it that the customer is often viewed as the enemy, rather than the competition? Some of this can be traced back to the early days, when production was the bottleneck and product demand was abundant.

Whenever a product is in short supply, the manufacturer becomes king and the customer is treated extremely poorly. Veteran sales-people who have experienced the days of product shortage have a hard time changing their attitude to the new world where there is enough production and not enough customers. There is also a certain sense of animosity against customers, as they so control the destiny of the salesperson. Every opportunity to get even is really cherished. Making the target is all that matters.

Many a sales manager has reduced the job of sales strategy to three simple words: 'Sell like hell'. This simple order has created more mayhem in many markets across the world than one can imagine. This is a call to arms and has an implicit understanding that orders be taken at any cost. What is not specified here is that rules can be bent if the situation gets out of hand. The other hidden message is that those who do not perform will go to hell. There is a certain feeling of do or die, and this stokes the salesperson to go out and do what it takes to safeguard the employment.

From such clarion calls have sales legends been born. Such was the case of Ravi Varma.

Ravi was a strong-built, aggressive person, with few choices in life. He had tried to be an engineer and didn't make the grade. He tried to be a lawyer and found it hard to read so much. Someone urged him to try being a salesperson.

He found that his personality was at times a bit hard for his customer to ignore. He realized that if he applied a particular tone of voice, he could overwhelm any resistance. He discovered that by applying an aggressive approach, he was often able to get more orders.

Soon the legend of Ravi grew and he was promoted to an area sales manager position. He realized now that he was the leader of a sales team and the same tactics that he had used to cow down customers were even more effective with the sales team. In one incident, Ravi came close to beating up a hapless salesperson who did not make his targets.

The magic seemed to be, in merely saying, 'Sell like hell'.

5

The Dowry Totem Pole

Dowry is a system, prevalent in India and parts of the Middle East, by which money and gifts are given at the time of marriage. While the bride's father gives the dowry in India, the bridegroom pays the 'bride money' in the Middle East. There are many social justifications for this practice and many ugly repercussions, especially among the poorer families.

An economic rationale for this system has also been the need to keep the family wealth within. Ostensibly, once a dowry has been paid, there is no claim on the family estate by the daughters of the family. Today, the law in India upholds the right of inheritance to daughters too. However, the practice is hard to legislate and continues, though not openly.

Social customs have a true assessment of how a person is valued in the society. There soon was a ready reckoner of sort and a pecking order of various professions. On top of the totem pole of dowry were doctors and engineers. Then came those who worked in the administration services of the country. Soon the pole was being climbed by the MBA, an upstart to fame and fortune, while mid-level of the totem pole was reserved for those with business acumen, the traders and entrepreneurs. As the nation developed, along with it did newer entrants such as those who immigrated to the promised lands such as Canada and the USA. A match who met the criterion was a proud one!

In the bazaars of India, the salesperson who most typifies the classical itinerant salesperson has been the medical rep or representative (MR). The community of MRs is a very curious one. They cluster together in the same hotels and have strict rules that everyone has to follow. So where on the totem pole does the lowly salesperson figure?

The dowry quoted for various professions, according to the market assessment, if indexed, could read something like this:

Doctors and engineers:	100
Government administrative services:	80
Business and entrepreneurs:	70
Green card holders:	70
Software technicians:	60
Lawyers/architects:	60
Salespeople:	45

Sales fraternity have realized that their worth on the lucrative marriage market is among the lowest. Of course, there were various reasons given for this such as a lower scholastic achievement, the rigours of travel and the one real unspoken reason, they cannot be trusted.

In fact, often in seedy hotel rooms where MRs flock, there are many jokes about how un-marriageable a salesperson is. One of the questions used to taunt the new salesperson is a stinging one: 'Would you allow your sister to marry a salesman?'

It is a sorry state when self-deprecating jokes are designed to confirm a lack of integrity as an acceptable standard. It indicates a situation beyond repair. There were days when a 'Made in India' stamp did little to promote the product. It forced unscrupulous manufacturers to rather stamp 'Made in USA', where the small print said that USA stood for 'United Sales Association'.

There is need for the profession to have a more acceptable reputation. This cannot happen if it is left to self-correct. Grave issues need positive action if there has to be any change. There has to be a concerted effort to correct a poor public image. It needs work to be done at the heart of the problem.

The intention is not to climb any dowry totem pole. It is to resurrect a profession that is maligned by a self-inflicted malaise.

The need to be trustworthy.

6

Ours Not to Reason Why

The concept of plenty is still a new one in many parts of the world. In other parts, there is no memory of shortage of goods. Many countries that were part of the erstwhile Soviet Union still have a hangover from the days when it was difficult to find sufficient goods. It was only when the Soviet Union crumbled that the East Bloc countries started experiencing the free flow of goods and services.

The most recent example of the contrast in Europe was the strange bifurcations of Germany after the Second World War. The Cold War made great fodder for stories of spies and the clandestine crossing of the Berlin Wall. This wall separated Germany and its people.

On 9 November 1989, the Berlin Wall came down and the contrast of the two economies was strident. It was also quite a statement on capitalism versus socialism. At the time of the Berlin Wall coming down, there were major shortages in East Germany.

Germany, which is known for producing some of the best luxury cars in the world, was divided into East Germany and West Germany until 1990. The former had a shortage of cars which were also of very poor quality. Appliances such as refrigerators and washing machines were hard to come by, and there were no luxury goods. Even supermarkets were few, and there were long queues in them.

Even as late as 2016, citizens of Venezuela shopped across the open borders of neighbouring Columbia to buy everyday grocery items. Food, medicine and cleaning products were in short supply. Salespeople, brought up in an economy of shortages, had a hard time adjusting to the new realities of plenty across the world.

Selling systems have to be modified to make the change that is required when the products are plenty. Often there is no time to make this change as the new economy of plenty charges forward. What does one do when suddenly the depots are full and customers are few? Most salespeople keep doing what they know best, be aggressive, like Ravi Varma was.

Unfortunately, Ravi Varma and his kind defined and managed sales values of this generation in transition. They successfully defined the norms. If bullying and misrepresentation worked for Ravi in the shortage years, why not continue more of the same? Aggression and bluster make poor substitutes for real strategic thinking.

This transition to a market of plenty did not happen overnight and salespeople continued to leverage those products still in short supply and dump the products which had few customers. A major in the business of selling batteries that are used in torches, wall clocks and transistor radios used the short supply and demand of its batteries to stuff hapless trade with torches that would have no takers.

In one such market, a distributor pushed cases of unsaleable torches just so he could place his battery order. The poor man had no buyer to sell these flashlights. So he broke up the torches and sold it to torch repair shops as spare parts.

This did not seem to faze the salesperson who was convinced that the customer overall made up the loss. This kind of reasoning supports all the wrong beings inflicted on the customer. Dumping is justified and repeated, often times until the customer collapses.

The damage done is never visible until after the dust settles. These practices maim not only the customer but also the market equity of the product. There are examples replete of how in one sales district the market share is low, while in the adjoining district the product is the dominant one. An analysis will reveal that the negligent behaviour of the salesperson in nurturing the sales territory had, over the years, brought about the downfall.

Such actions destroy even the future of the brand in the markets. Holding the posterity of the brand to ransom just for meeting the month's sales figures is a very short-sighted and reckless decision.

7

Pirates of Sales:
The Story of Medical Reps

One of the largest sales teams in any country are the MRs of the pharmaceutical industry.

The MRs, as they are known, have a really rigid work day. They can only determine when to start the day. When the day ends depends on the doctor they plan to visit. Doctors have a very dismissive attitude to the gathering bunch of reps that wish to call on them. At times, they are made to wait in the doctor's waiting room until all the patients are handled by the doctor.

There is a doctor in Nagpur, who is known to make all sales reps wait until midnight when he has completed seeing all his patients. He then calls all of them to enter his chamber and gets them all to place their free samples on his table. He then allows them to say a few words recommending their product and sends them all away.

In a pharmaceutical company, the prescribing doctor plays the main role in the business plan. It is the joint effort of the marketing and sales team to bring out a new marketing plan each year. New product launches are planned, but these hardly account for the major areas of sales activity such as new detailing methods and new scientific issues which form a basis of discussion between the medical sales rep and the doctor.

Nothing comes close to the efforts that are reserved for CRM—customer relationship management. A very sophisticated name for a rather shameful activity which could better have been called a 'customer gratification programme'. Pharmaceutical companies are keen to sponsor international meets for the medical community. They are also happy to organize free medical camps and promotion of inter-medical college festivals. However, all these are a veneer for the really effective campaigns. Doctors receive customized high-value gifts which act as brand reminders.

Recently, there have been foreign tours of sightseeing with no effort to couch it with any scientific input.

There are holiday tours to international locations for the doctors and their families. How objective or impartial can a doctor be after such a holiday to prescribe without an ulterior motive?

Doctors are also gifted white goods such as air conditioners and office equipment. While medical councils have tried to stop these practices, there is very little impact.

Product innovation plays a very important part in the health industry. However, to launch something absolutely new is hard for every pharmaceutical company. When product innovation is poor, the gifting to doctors increases so as to compensate. Very few pharmaceutical companies look beyond the doctor and at the patient.

When the company supports such blatant efforts to win over market share, can the MR be a silent spectator? Not really; they too have their cut.

8

More Pirates of Sales:
Dumping Sales

It was year-ending and there was a hush over the Bombay (now Mumbai) sales branch. Everyone walked around like expectant fathers outside a maternity ward. This was the month when there has to be no missing the quota. The sales of the final month sealed the Annual Report. There was an overall sense of foreboding.

C.M. Mathew had taken over the branch as branch manager only three months previously. For the first time he was a metro branch head. He was keen to show that he was capable. The markets were tepid. There were stocks flowing unabated from lower sales tax states like Delhi. It looked like really tough going.

Bombay metro was under a raw MBA, Rohan, who had found the volatile market flows of grey market extremely unnerving. Mathew knew if Bombay did not meet its target, there would be little chance of the branch meeting its commitment to head office (HO). He wondered if he had been wise to keep the old fox Rusi Canteenwala away from Bombay city sales. Too late, he felt. He just hoped that there would not have to be recourse to dumping the trade.

'Dumping' was a practice Mathew detested. This is when stocks are shipped without an order, to the distributor, often without prior information. This has longer-term repercussion. Being the year-end, the trade too were prepared with apprehension for such an eventuality. It happened every year. When Rohan walked into the branch manager's cabin, Mathew prepared for the worst.

Bombay metro was only 60 per cent of the estimate. Rohan looked desperate. The market prices had crashed, he reported, with year-end distress sales happening all across the neighbouring states. Just then Rusi walked in looking quite smug. He was responsible for Maharashtra up-country sales. He slapped a bunch of order sheets on Mathew's table. On target, he said. Seeing Rohan's despondence, he asked how the metro sales went.

Rusi had previously looked after metro and was known to the trade there. Seeing an opportunity, he asked Mathew if he could try his hand at selling to the distributors of the city. Mathew was caught between breaking protocol and reporting bad news to the HO. He asked Rohan if he minded. With the branch honour at stake, he had little choice but to agree.

It was the longest three hours before Rusi returned, all smiles, and declared to Mathew that he had completed the shortfall and booked more orders! There were commendations all around and Rohan was farther in the dumps. How come, he wondered, that his sales team was unable to do what Rusi had accomplished so skilfully? It was then that the phones started ringing.

Rohan listened with disbelief as his sales team reported that Rusi had been to the main distributors in the wholesale market and had promised that a special discount to offset the low open market prices would be clandestinely given to the trade.

This could not be officially given as all sales discounts were centrally controlled by the HO. Rusi had asked the trade to prepare fake claims of defective products. Rohan was determined that he would not be a party to this fraud. He told Rusi that whatever had been promised the trade, he would have to settle that from his zone. When Rusi heard it, he shouted and cursed and said that he was not able to settle metro claims through upcountry sales. Rohan's team immediately informed the distributors that the deal was off.

In the space of the few hours, some of the distributors had already booked about 50 per cent of the stock they had ordered with Rusi, anticipating the delivery the following day. They pressed Rohan to settle the claim. Mathew washed his hands off the whole deal as he knew that Rusi had worked without official sanction.

Dumping is a sales malpractice that nearly always ends with grief. It is the last-minute desperation with promises to make it right the following month. It sours trade relations and could end with serious damage to the trade, the brand and even the company. It kills the bottom line.

9

Even More Pirates of Sales

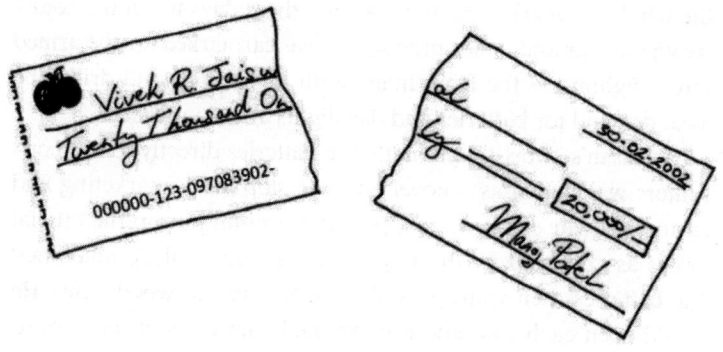

Salespeople have a lot to cope with. It is not just the hostile markets and canny competition. Sometimes, the enemy is from within. The damage that happens in such a situation is hard to anticipate, often years before it is known.

As it happened with the curious case of the obeisant distributor, Harkisan Ramnath, the powerful distributor in one of the most volatile markets of UP, Kanpur.

The old-world distributors had seen the days of shortage of product and the line of eager consumers who would line-up each morning as Harkisan opened his unimposing shop in the heart of the wholesale market. He remembered those days when the country was at war and major production was earmarked for the armed forces fighting at the front lines. With nightly air-raid drills, the local demand for batteries and flashlights also skyrocketed.

Harkisan's effort to distribute the batteries directly to the consumers was hailed as a novel effort to stop black marketing and ensure the war effort was supported. Harkisan put up the official prices as approved by the Department of Essential Commodities. The batteries then were packed in strong mango wood cases. He would open each case and remove the batteries from the cartons and sell not more than four pieces to each consumer lined up. Harkisan was lauded by the company and his initiative mentioned in the company house journal. What a nice guy he was!

Of course, what was not known was that on each sale to the consumer, Harkisan made not only his own distributor margin, but also the retailer's margin. He also sold these wooden crates. After the war was over, Harkisan built a very smart bungalow which he called 'Crater Villa'. He would proudly tell his guests that the building was totally funded by the sale of the wooden crates.

Kanpur and Harkisan continued to be among the most favoured distributors, even when times got tough. He was always ready to help out the company salesperson's target shortfall. Sales team members were always envious of the salesperson who had Harkisan as a distributor. Kanpur became extremely important, and it showed in the national sales achievement.

Those were the days before the banking system improved and long before electronic banking came into being. The payment system at each sales branch was to keep signed blank cheques in every branch office so that as the shipment was made from the depot, the cheque was dropped for the exact amount. As it took sometimes even a month for the cheque to be credited, the State Bank of India had a facility, whereby they would underwrite the cheques deposited anywhere in India and give immediate credit. Naturally, for a small fee. It seemed to work well enough and everyone was pleased, especially Harkisan.

It was some seven years later that in an internal audit of the State Bank, a strange phenomenon was discovered. The bank found a discrepancy in the reconciliation of the company's account. There appeared to be millions of rupees missing. The bank raised a debit note on the company for about ₹400 million. The company did their own investigation and discovered that strangely, all the cheques deposited by the mega Kanpur distributor had never been presented to his bank for payment. Harkisan claimed to be unaware of such a situation and offered to cooperate in the investigation.

Oddly, the cheques seemed to have all been lost in transit from the State Bank of India to his branch of Kisan Cooperative Bank. Years of investigations carried on and finally it was found that an errant bank employee, who had since died under strange circumstances, had diligently torn all the cheques that had been sent by the State Bank. Harkisan offered to make good the lost cheques. He requested that he be allowed adequate time to collect the funds.

Harkisan was a gentleman to the end. Sadly, the end came sooner than he could complete the repayment.

10

Still More Pirates of Sales

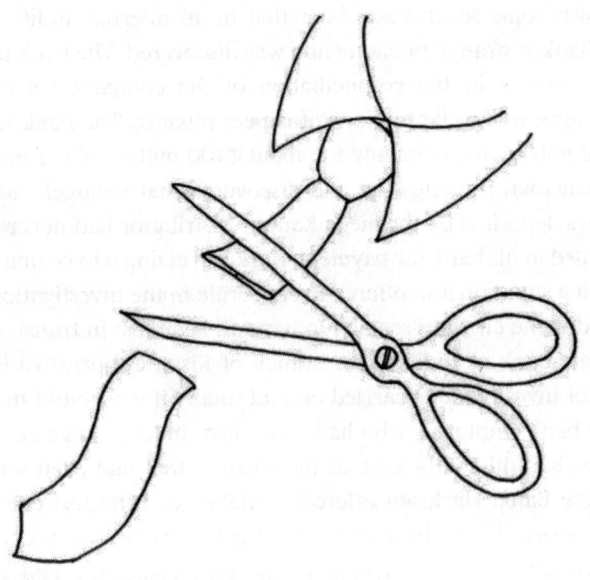

The salesperson operates quite by remote control. So much is dependent on the trust that is placed on each team member. Self-regulation is hard to do for the best of individuals. There is something that snaps while on tour.

At times the work is so tiring that just pushing one out of bed is a challenge. Every time the journey cycle is complete, the family descends and starts to demand the pent-up attention deficit. There were times when a salesperson set out on a tour that could last 45 days. One can hardly imagine what stress this causes to both the family and the individual.

In the 1970s, the tour cycle was down to 22 days per month, with a day of rest after every 11 days. This too became hard to implement. Home every weekend was the goal. Today, there are situations when even a three-day tour programme is considered a bit extreme.

Perhaps the unnatural design of traditional sales travel could account for the amount of lies and misrepresentation that are part of everyday sales world. There are many simple and elaborate ploys to avoid detection.

There have been salespeople on tour who have never reached their destination as they just decided to play hooky and keep it a secret that they were not at their post. There is severe punishment for those caught. Yet the urge to falsify their daily report is hard to resist.

Even after reaching the upcountry markets, there are many options to being at work. Many steal away, after lunch, to their hotel rooms for a cosy siesta or a matinee in a remote cinema hall, who is to know? The problem is rampant in pharmaceutical sales too.

In the pharma industry, the MR is measured by many parameters, one of which is the daily call list, also known as the 'doctor list'. This call list is mandatory to be submitted. In truth, it is very hard to ensure that the doctor was really called on. Often the doctors that run a clinic ask the MRs to wait until every patient has been attended to. This is really a drag, and it takes some extraordinary commitment to be waiting in a stuffy waiting room with other MRs. Daily call sheets are fudged and physicians samples misused.

In certain towns of Punjab, there were associations of MRs whose sole purpose was to protect the MRs from being spied on by the boss. They made rules that no surprise visit by senior officers could be permitted without prior information to the association office. One such boss ignored this directive and paid dearly for it.

As he arrived in the town, he was greeted by the association members who marched him straight to the office and asked him to explain how he had hoped to ignore the directive. After detaining him for the whole day, without food, drink or hygiene breaks, he was permitted to catch the evening train back after a formal function, when his tie was cut with a pair of scissors and the severed part of the tie pinned to the wall like a trophy.

He was given a stern warning that, if repeated, their response would be less gentlemanly!

Travel expenses are always a happy hunting ground for every internal auditor. There are many ways that the expenses are 'modified' or simply fabricated. A typical effort involves booking a train ticket in air-conditioned class, as permitted by the travel rules, but travelling by ordinary second class. With railways going for online booking, this became even easier as all they have to do is book and cancel the ticket later. The original ticket is attached as proof in the expense report. It is hard to really check if the journey was ever completed.

Variation of this was to travel by bus and to claim having travelled by taxi. In the area of food, fudging bills are not uncommon. Of course, companies take severe action, including removing them from employment, yet the scourge persists. There are many justifications for this subterfuge. The company was not charged more than the policy. If the salesperson suffered the discomfort and travelled in a cheaper class, is he not entitled to enjoy the saving he had made?

With corruption a way of life, it is sometimes difficult to convince those committing the breach that the conduct was deserving of such retribution.

11

The Heroes of Sales

Salespeople are subject to bad press. It does not mean that all salespeople are to be washed in shame. There are some who are considered 'heroes'. Despite the conditions that make it easy being dishonest and untrustworthy, there are those who simply do not succumb to pressure of any kind.

Sorbhoni Ghosh was not the everyday salesperson. She was known all over the Eastern India. She looked every bit the disarming housewife. Slightly greying at the temples, she had a charming way of handling customers. She, being a lady in selling, was always a surprise that went very positively for her meeting customers. She had a quality that would have stood her in good stead, if she ever was to be a doctor: she seemed to be in no hurry and made the customer feel special.

Sorbhoni had a talent to zero in on the real needs of each customer. When the customer signed the order, the feeling was that Sorbhoni had done the customer a good turn. Once a customer, there was no way except to give a positive referral. Even those who had no need for hospital furniture knew of her.

There was power in her word. A commitment from Sorbhoni was likened to the promise of the Reserve Bank on each currency note. She could be very assertive and when dealing with her own company, she was a Bengal tigress, fighting for the rights of her customers. The plant at Gujarat gave her orders special treatment. They too would not cross her when she wanted service urgently for her customers.

The curious part was that her pricing was always higher than the national average. Credit was strictly within the norms. It was whispered that she had walked out of a negotiation with a major hospital simply because they wanted to include terms that could be evading taxes. She saw life in black and white, not shades of grey.

Sorbhoni could never speak ill of any customer, even if they refused her an order. She had a thick diary into which she put in all that she discussed with the customer. Without that well-worn leather bound book, she was at a loss. She never trusted anyone with her precious diary. The younger sales team members would tease her that long before Steve Jobs had the iPad, Sorbhoni had her own laptop, her trusty diary. She claimed it was superior as it never hanged, ran out of juice or cracked on dropping!

Sorbhoni was a role model to the rest of the sales team. Many a visitor to Kolkata from HO tried to discover her secret of success. All they could see was that if she had fixed an appointment, there was no question of being late. She set her watch 10 minutes faster to ensure that she would arrive ahead of the scheduled time.

It was interesting to see that every meeting with the customer would be light conversation on anything but the business at hand. Only when she felt the mood was right would she open up the business part of the meeting. She would have a barrage of questions and it appeared at times that she had forgotten to ask for the order. Often, she would murmur that she was not sure she had a correct solution for the customer's need. She would ask for time to confer with her plant and R&D people before she could offer any product.

The HO people would worry if such an approach would lose her the order. Sorbhoni was never in a hurry. She knew that the order was hers for the taking when she was ready for it. Sure enough, in time the order would arrive, neatly stitched up.

Sorbhoni was always ready to learn anything new. She would have a very eager look on her face and an intent to assimilate that would warm the heart of any trainer. In time, there was a joint venture with one of the leading hospital furniture companies in the USA. Sorbhoni was asked to visit the plants in various parts of the world to lead the campaign to bring in high-end products from the joint venture partner.

When it came to hang up her diary and retire, she was asked to carry on and be on a retainer. Her contact with customers and the deep relationships she built could not be jeopardized by her retirement. She happily continues to do what she loves best, sharing stories of her life with her grandchildren Anousha and Avi.

A true sales icon, with no compromise.

12

Why Do Salespeople Lie?

There are those who say that no one in the world goes without taking recourse to lies—white lies, minor lies, major lies and outright con jobs. Yet not all professions carry the burden of being generally untruthful. There may be other professions that might give a run for the money on the sweepstakes of being the most deceitful. The concern is not with them. Why do salespeople lie?

Social scientist, Bella DePaulo, a psychologist and affiliate of the University of California, has studied lies and why people choose to do so. She has figured that there are two categories of lies. The first is self-serving (told to advantage the liar or protect the liar from embarrassment, blame or other undesired outcomes) and the other is to be kind (told to advantage, flatter or protect some else). DePaulo defines, 'A lie occurs anytime you intentionally mislead someone'. The college students in the research told an average of two lies a day and non-students told one.

A more recent study of the lies 1,000 US adults told in the previous 24 hours found that people told an average of 1.65 lies per day: the authors noted that 60 per cent of the participants said that they told no lies at all, while the top 5 per cent of liars told nearly half of all falsehoods in the study.

The nature of the sales chain of command has always been very military. There is an attitude that each day is a battle day. The market is the war zone and every day is one of combat. Most sales managers assume the role of the drill sergeant. Orders are barked and compliance is assumed. There is one difference.

Sales teams are unlike army platoons that march into every campaign together and fight as one unit. The sales team is dispersed and each one operates on their own. Once the team leaves the sales meeting called by the sales manager, they are no longer under the direct gaze of the boss. Much then is left to their own sense of responsibility.

Douglas McGregor expounded the Theory X and Theory Y understanding of motivation. McGregor argued that the level of maturity of each individual determines the manner of how the person is supervised. The 'X' type of maturity indicated a low level of development, requiring close monitoring and the need for giving direction. Very much like how a mother deals with a young child.

The 'Y' type is more evolved in maturity. They can be relied on to self-regulate, do what is right and require less supervision. A sales team is a mix of both 'X' and 'Y'. It can be projected that the propensity to fib is greater with the 'X' type. Or so it appears.

The military bearing of sales also projects an attitude that what the sergeant major does not see or misses is par for the course. School boys in boarding schools have this same attitude. Everything is okay as long as one does not get caught. There is often a phrase in the sales world that modifies the adage 'Honesty is the best policy' to the more relevant one 'Honesty is the best policy, when there is no policy left'.

So why do salespeople lie?

In a survey of senior sales managers, some of the insights are as follows:

- Sudhir Chand, director on Exide Industries India Ltd board, a marketing whiz who shepherded the car battery sales to a pre-eminent position, says, 'Perhaps for the same reason that everyone who lies does. They want to look good while not being ready to go the whole mile, and earn what makes them look good'.

- Askok Jaidka, retired chairman, Asia Pacific for Hellman, a major European freight company, says, 'It is easier to lie than to work hard. There is also the belief that the bosses have little knowledge of the on-ground reality, to know if what is being reported is a lie or the truth'.

- Ravi Swaminathan, ex MD, AMD and considered one of the main movers of personal computers in India while with Compac and Hewlet Packard, has this to say,

Sales people are not all given to lying but the line between the truth and the order is a slim one. They look at truth as one of perception rather than an absolute black and white proposition. If a customer is better served with a version of the truth, they are not going to be rigid and unbending.

• David Adams, previously head of Human Resources with Dexion, UK, considers bending the truth a very universal tactic. While buyers are told 'caveat emptor' before every important purchase, in every selling situation the seller's judgement is challenged by four temptations:

  • It is easier to fool unsuspecting people than to serve them.
  • It takes less courage to hide the truth than to admit it.
  • It takes less time to lie than to build trust.
  • It is easier to conceal the truth than to uncover deception.

• Akash Abraham, sales head for specialty sales, BASF, based out of New Jersey, has a more global perspective as he travels widely on his work,

    Yes, one always has to be aware that the full truth is not necessary all the time. However, it is not to be used without restraint. People, across the world, look poorly on those who lie even occasionally. They lie because they are not 'good enough'.

Across the survey, it appeared that the base of all lying is the reluctance to face up the possibility of failure. It seems to be the most common motivation to lie: Fear.

White lies, minor and major lies and downright whoppers, all have the same source. So, who are they who tell the truth? Those who are confident of who and what they are. Those who don't see failure as the end of the world. Those who have failed before and learned from the experience.

Is it possible that a lack of knowledge and ability, among salespeople, is why so many recourse to lying?

13

To Be a Professional Salesperson

The word 'professional' is loosely used today. Everyone claims to be one, little understanding the obligations of such a tag.

A professional is one who has been formally trained and guided to understand the subject of expertise along with the skills that will make the practice accredited. Often there are bodies that define and certify the expertise. The purpose is to avoid charlatans and quacks charade as genuine practitioners. There is more to being a professional than just this.

A true professional is committed not only to the discipline and rigour as laid forth by those who certify but also to the guiding principles that are not negotiable. The medical profession has very clearly laid out the theory and practice of medicine which also bound the membership to a set of values called the 'Hippocratic Oath'. Sales lack any such regime.

Over 50 years ago, a young and ambitious salesperson named Jack Carew found that he had the magic wand that made sales happen. He really could not put a fix on what it was that he did which caused this to happen. Interestingly, when he moved to another territory, the person replacing him did not have the same sales results.

He was also upset with the poor image salespeople had across industries. He decided to do something about it. Jack realized that to make a real difference, one needed to understand the process of a sale before one could start defining sales universals.

Jack decided to study the work that his sales team members did to complete their sales. In fact, he put a university professor to study the sales process used. To their surprise, there appeared to be no common process, each doing whatever it took to get an order. He also noted that salespeople said anything to support their claims. He set about to do his bit to rectify this.

He worked to study the consumer, and to understand what the drivers are that impact a buying decision. He argued that once this was clear, making a sale was easy and within the benefit of what the customer needs. From this quest was born the seminal work called the Dimensions of Professional Selling (DPS).

Jack argues that selling is a talent everyone is born with, similar to the ability to sing a song. If one were to watch a kindergarten class in progress, when the teacher announces that it is 'singing time', there is a shout of approval and many little hands shoot up to be the first to sing. Each of the little pupils feels capable of singing. Fast forward to the same group of kids, now adults, and announce the same message, 'it's sing-along time', and watch so many claim they can't sing. Education possibly ruined the innate talent.

Sales too is a skill everyone uses, some better than others. It is hard to identify a single person, in history or alive today, that never had to use the skill of selling. A mother of a newly born manages extremely well with no verbal communication. Spiritual leaders are great salespeople. Politicians have to be good at it. No one can duck this.

Unlike the talent to sing which needs coaching to sing at a professional level, there are few or no real efforts to bring sales under a discipline. Everyone tries what they think is the best way to improve their sales capability. While this may pass at the individual level, it is a ticking time bomb when a company fails to recognize the need to professionalize its sales team.

Sales training that emphasizes form over substance does just that.

14

Who Teaches Whom to Sell?

Each profession draws a certain type of person. The armed forces keep physical fitness as a prime requirement when they recruit. Recently, a video went viral where a little boy, Mateo, has an engaging negotiation with his mother who refuses to give him cupcakes for dinner. Over 3.5 million watched the video, including the talk show host Ellen DeGeneres.

She was so taken in by little Mateo's ability to push his case that she called him on her show in hopes that he would grow and join her legal team. After all, don't we need lawyers who are argumentative people? So, what kind of a person makes the best salesperson?

'Talkative' seems to win by a long shot. Which salesperson will not gain with the gift of the gab? A good personality is the next popular requirement. Following close, after that, is the ability to be creative. No harm there, if it is focused on new ways to sell. However, the creativity is expected to extend to where truth abides.

So the understanding of sales is based on some hackneyed understanding of what it takes to sell well. Having hired such a person, companies go about trying to train them into the selling job, here again, without really understanding what to teach. The induction programme is all that is served out to the recruit.

There are many companies that believe that a solid introduction into the technical aspects of the product is the only injection required to churn out an excellent salesperson. There are plant visits, time spent in the R&D laboratory and anything that is necessary to fill the gaps of product knowledge. This is rightly so.

Commercial knowledge is the other area of induction training. This too is a very important part of preparing a salesperson for the nitty-gritty of the market. There is also a mandatory section on distribution, trade margins, return on investment and policies that cover activity in the field. Reporting from the market, competitive information and, of course, expense reports and travel benefits too constitute an important part of induction training.

And how does one sell? This is considered already covered in the technical session. If you know your product well, where is the need for any selling? The customer will be thrilled to buy as soon as they hear all the technical advantages of the product. It is interesting that even the Japanese have little concern for how to sell. Professor Banteru Kurahara of the Union of Japanese Scientist and Engineers (JUSE), an authority of Total Quality Management, on a visit to India, was quizzed how the total quality programme could be incorporated into sales, but he had little to offer. He offered that if you do everything else right by total quality management (TQM), the product will be its own salesperson. In short, no one really knows what to say about the skill of selling, except to hand over a sales kitbag to the salespeople and kick them into the market.

Most companies have an easy way of farming out training to the senior salesperson. Shadow the sales expert and learn by observation. A little overlooked fact, no one ever gave the expert a formal lesson on how to sell. Most MBA programmes skirt sales with a few dry chapters on distribution. Market dynamics and how to handle the customer are really not touched on.

The recruit who is thrown into the market watches the senior sales master and wonders how or when he would have such a rapport with customers and would he ever be able to sell? Here is the beginning of the lack of confidence. As they grow from the position of the beginner, to novice, to intermediate, then advanced and finally the master, each person develops a pattern of how to deal with the lack of an approved sales system. As confidence withers, the propensity to twist the truth increases. This is not restricted to a few nations.

In Britain too, many sales staff are poorly trained and therefore regularly accused of insufficient knowledge of the products they sell. They are also ignorant of sales psychology. Sales training in all its fields is seriously lacking in the UK and has been so for some years. The word 'service' is not understood. The time and attention often given to customers in North America is much better, and 'service' in this context means helping and assisting the customer to buy, not neglecting or ignoring them!

Until there is a clear understanding of how one is to approach a customer, how to engage in conversation, how to find out why he will buy and how to make a pitch with sales impact, there is no real discipline of selling. So many salespeople just put off the customer with the first contact.

Professional selling and a selling system, relevant to the particular industry, are necessary first steps in making salespeople confident and trustworthy. This is not hard and can be done with so much of relevance to the market challenges.

15

The Sins of Our Forefathers

'Dumping' is a word that has a deep resonance with all companies that have a tier system of distribution. This is not common in industrial products where the factory is the mode of selling to the final user. Dumping on the final user is rarely possible and is immediately noticed and aborted. It is quite the other way, where fast moving consumer goods (FMCG) are concerned.

The traditional FMCG method of distribution has a three-tier level of selling. The first level is from the manufacturer to the distributor. This is often referred to as the primary sale. The goods at this stage are paid for and await sale to the next level. When this sale happens, it could be from the distributor to the sub-stockist. This movement could be termed as the secondary sale.

The final sale is to the consumer, and this is considered the tertiary sale. How does the design of the distribution impact the propensity to 'dump'? Each level is a point where inventory can be held. It matters little if the product is paid for or not. The more the levels, where inventory is stored, the greater the chance there is that it can be misused. All inventory in excess of the tertiary movement of a product is a drag on the velocity of money invested in the business.

In one FMCG company, the practice of dumping stocks with the trade was formal every year-end. Year-end loading is common in most companies. However, the practice becomes pernicious with each year. For instance, if a company sold 30 per cent more in one year-end, it immediately meant that the new year's potential was less to that extent and extra targets for the year. At the second-year closing, the pressure for dumping grows greater. So the excess loaded in the second year becomes 50 per cent more than normal sales.

This company found themselves in a corner every year as the previous year's oversell forced the management to dump even more the following year. It got to a point that they found themselves at one year-ending loading exactly 100 per cent more than an average monthly off-take. Practically speaking, this meant that the new year would only have 11 months of sale. No one was ready to bell the cat and correct the situation until finally the owner's son saw the danger and took a decision one year-ending to not oversell.

Results for the year were affected severely. It was handled, as it was a conscious management decision. Thereafter, there was a policy that year-end sales could not exceed the normal average. It greatly improved the sale and cash flow of the new year. Oft, the sins of the forefathers are visited on the generations that follow. It takes extraordinary courage to cut the Gordian knot as did Alexander the Great.

A connected problem to such acts of formal dumping by management is the dilution of the sin. The salesperson views that overselling, when promoted by management, is okay. When it is done by them, with no nod from management, can it be really that wrong?

Sales malpractice is the act of selling more than what a customer can normally consume for the given period of time. It is wrong and should not get sanctified by mere levels of management. It dilutes management's moral authority.

It happened in another company when sales went low and inventories started piling up, a sales promotion scheme was announced to give customers extra discounts on sales exceeding their previous year's average sales of the same period. The better one did than last year, the higher was the discount. This did not result in the expected sales.

Sales creativity was brought into play. Instead of invoicing Customer A, the sales branches, with the blessings of the head of sales, created a new firm as an allied firm of the Customer A. This new firm had no previous sales history and was happily invoiced at the highest discount. Customer A did not buy any in the same period. Internal audit identified the 'interrelated party' sales and declared the sales 'infructuous'.

There is a real danger to the profession when sales management encourages sales malpractice or turns a blind eye when sales policies are overturned with impunity. This really ends with management losing all moral authority. Even worse is when senior sales management speak with forked tongue, as Native Americans would say. When the scam is public, they take the moral high ground and punish those who get caught, at times even having them sacked.

Truly, the sins of seniors are atoned for by the juniors.

16

Understanding the Nature of a Sale

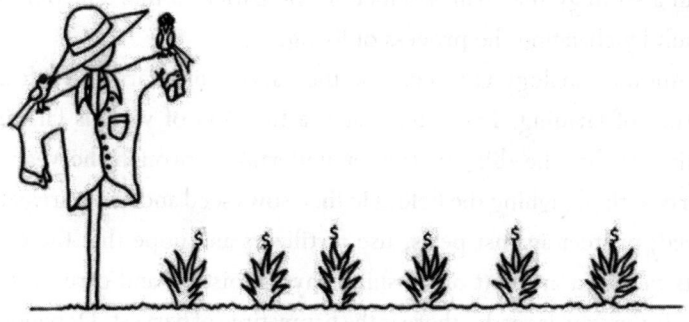

A common question asked at every sales training programme is: 'What is a sale?' Even when asked of veteran salespeople, the answers are varied and not clear. There is definitely no common understanding. It gets worse if one were to ask, 'What is the process of a sale?'

Often, salespeople identify with only the final act of booking an order and getting the payment. Sales results are just that—only results, quite akin to the lab reports that one gets when the doctor orders some blood tests. Each person's blood reports reflect a lifestyle and the functioning of the various parts of the body and its organs. As people vary in the way they live, eat or drink, their reports are rarely alike. The results give the doctor the direction to plan a strategy that will produce in the patient a more favourable result by changing the process of living.

Another analogy is to confuse the harvest of a farmer with the nature of farming. Every harvest is a function of various farming activities that the diligent farmer undertakes through the year. It starts with ploughing the field. He then sows seed and has to irrigate, weed, protect against pests, use fertilizers and hope that the crop gets the right amount of sunshine days, moisture and care. When finally the crop is ready, there is the happy time of harvest. Depending on the system of farming, he gets the results of his toil.

If the harvest was below the expectation, a review is done to ensure that the harvest the following year meets the targets. No farmer worth his salt would leave his fields to the vagaries of nature and turn up only at cropping time. Yet this is what salespeople seem to do. They assemble at month-end and start to call up on the phone potential customers on whom they can dump material. Perhaps, if there was a sales system which was piously followed, there would be no need to hustle at month-end.

Why is there no regard for a system among sales teams? Sales policies do not substitute for a sales process. When no process is defined, there is scope for everyone to do what they like. When members of the sales team follow their heart and get sales come what may, mayhem comes. So, what really comprises a sales process?

The essence of a sales process is to know how a customer goes about deciding on what to buy. This is the Holy Grail of the salesperson's quest, to know what moves her to buy. Easy to say, but it is hard to do it. Most sales trainers believe that there are certain minimum actions to be completed and the order is in the bag. There really is a step-by-step process. Knowing this gives the salesperson the confidence that the task of making a sale is not just bravado but also a system of doing a job right, every time.

Most robust sales training programmes talk of this delicate process. In the Huthwaite Groups' SPIN Selling system, by Neil Rackam, there are four simple stages in the selling process.

The first is to ask 'Situation' questions. This is to have salespeople ask the customer for information of facts that will give a lead to locate a customer's potential problem area. An example is 'Please tell me what the situation you face today is.'

The next step is to identify the 'Problem' with a question like 'How often does this happen?'

The third step is the 'Implication' question. Here the salesperson tries to assess the extent of impact the problem has if not solved. An example is 'How much has this problem affected you, in productivity or cost?'

The fourth and last part of the SPIN Selling system tries 'Needs Pay-off' question. Here the salesperson tries to assess the benefit to the customer, with the problem being solved.

There are critics of the SPIN process of selling, but it is robust and clearly lays out a path for understanding the nature of sales. Carew International, USA, has the classic Positional Selling process, yet another effort to establish a process of selling that will make this a profession. More about that is discussed in the chapters ahead.

17

Sales Is Relationship at Work

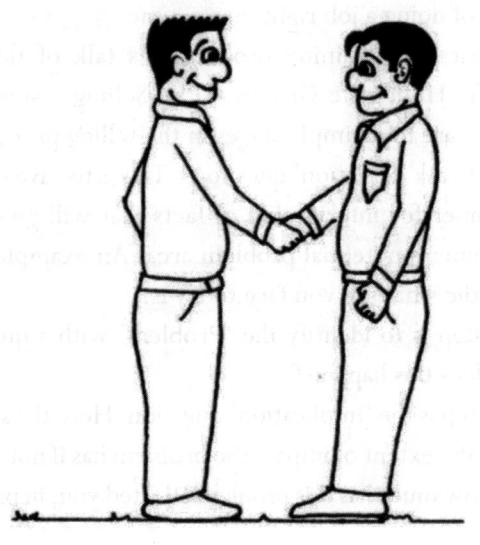

Sales and sales teams have a hard-to-ignore aspect. It all has to do with relationship building. In the chronology of sales, the first formal retail effort has been the friendly mom-and-pop store. The last hundred years have seen developments in retail that boggle the mind.

According to the existing knowledge, retail markets and shops have a very ancient history dating back over 10,000 years. Over the centuries, the little store grew to be malls, to the amazing malls and hypermarkets. Many a tear has been shed for the small-time retailer whose demise has been loudly acclaimed.

The juggernaut of modern retail has been blamed for the decreasing number of kiosks and small shops. Yet there seems to be no country that can claim to have done away with this form of serving customers with a 'sale in small quantities', taken from the old French word *tailler*, which subsequently became 'retailer' in French, Dutch and German. Why is it hard to exterminate the small-time retailer?

There is an iconic market in Kolkata named after an Englishman called S.S. Hogg. It was called Hogg Market until it became the never-aging 'New Market'. This was one of the earliest malls in India and to this date is dearly loved by anyone who is fortunate to live in Kolkata. Here one can buy anything one fancies, from Chinese shoes, to luggage, to lemon tarts at Nahoums, to beef, mutton, chicken and all that a supermarket carries.

Many of the old shoppers of New Market have immigrated to Australia, Canada and other countries. Come December, there is an influx of returning Indians who want a Kolkata Christmas, like it used to be. These denizens of the advanced economies are used to all the modern retail wonders. Nothing, but nothing compares to a walk down the many aisles of Hogg market. Not for what is sold, but to be remembered by the old shopkeepers by name and to savour the unblemished sweetness of an old relationship. Yes, they shamelessly return for the warmth of the welcoming 'hello'. Maybe, they are also there for the Christmas cake and the traditional corned beef.

Look at what has happened to retail ever since Jeff Bezos turned retailer. Retail will never be the same again with online sales getting amazingly popular. Amazon, Flipkart, Myntra and even Alibaba from China are household names now.

> In remote Udaipur, a young teenager called Anjali looks at a piece of costume jewellery she ordered online from Alibaba, with the total invoice price not exceeding $0.60. It costs more to post a letter from China to India. Here is the wonder of this new way to shop. Yet this transaction is a faceless one. Neither the buyer nor the seller ever meet. How does one substitute for the loss of 'hail-fellow-well-met'?

In the era of Amazon and others, is there any chance to develop the relationship side of personal selling? Or is the day of the sales team over? In this age of literature in 140 digits, does anyone care to read more, shake a hand or simply drop in to have a cup of coffee (no business, please!)? Or is 10,000 years of a good thing too much to endure anymore?

Siri and Cortina are very efficient and can do amazing things, yet in any sale that is a continuous, long-term one, there is still the enormous power of the salesperson's ability to respond to a customer's real and implicit needs. Nothing quite has replaced it. It also explains the ease with which Amazon India, a late starter, covered ground and caught up with the leader Flipkart. Today, it has overtaken the leader. Yes deep pockets do help, but looked clinically, there was no real bond with Flipkart that made it hard to overcome competition.

A lot has been written about how the salesperson today has to move up from solution providing to being as savvy as the Internet-bred consumer. There are many changes in the style of selling which are relevant to the changing consumer. There is no substitute to unearthing the real need of the consumer, especially when the consumer is not clear about his/her own needs.

Relationships make all the difference to sales. Trust makes all the difference to the quality of relationships developed in sales.

18

The Lonely Salesperson

Across the world, after a really hectic day, the salesperson checks into the regular hotel and proceeds to spend the evening alone. Journey cycles now have become easier, and the instant communication through the mobile phone makes keeping in touch with home simple. It has never been so good.

In the early glory days, the salesperson left on a journey cycle of about a month, returning home to find that lots of life had passed by in the time in between. Children falling sick, small emergencies that required attention and the seething sense of despair as one's spouse tries to do everything and yet keep sane. The money is never enough.

Conversations with one's direct boss while on tour rarely leave one feeling charged up. There are things to improve and the sales results that 'just won't do'. The promise of the bright tomorrow is: 'Keep on this like this and don't blame me for what happens'.

The day in the market is sometimes a repetitive litany of refusals. The sundown is the best part of the day. Drag one's weary bones to the little hotel room that still stinks of the tobacco, smoked by the previous resident. Take a shower and then work on the daily reports that no one reads.

The noise from the adjoining room tells of a raucous gathering of salespeople from other companies. The laughter, though unintended, mocks the life of a man no one wants to know or care about. There is always the consolation in the friar of Mohan Nagar, the ever amiable, Old Monk. The realms of spirituality thus attained cast a pall on reality.

Many in sales are hard drinkers. Initially, it is to take the stress off the nerves, and gradually it becomes a world of make believe, where every problem is left in a nether world. It is a space, where saying it, as it is, needs no thought. Say it like how one sees it. This explains how, when the faithful assemble for the annual sales conference, so many hard truths are spilled during the cocktail hour, also a time when many a career is jettisoned to the comforting allure of the night spirits.

The working day is full of people who are just associates and passing acquaintances. It is the same feeling one gets at the CST (earlier VT) station in Mumbai as the tsunami of office-goers flow incessantly out. In the midst of such a crowd, the lonely can feel no comfort. Stay there long enough and reality slips away until one cannot trust any feeling that surfaced.

Something similar happens on a long sales tour. All reality checks are subject to the scorching scrutiny of one's own perspective. Small issues get magnified and the salesperson is beset by imaginings. A peculiar undertone in the boss' voice, detected in the afternoon's conversation, can be the trigger to an unrealistic panic attack as night falls. The spirits of the night further deepen the depression.

During one such night, Sunil Gupta, a sales rep, who worked with a multinational pharma group, received an ominous call from his sales manager. In it was a straight accusation of monetary impropriety. Sunil's immediate resignation was demanded over the phone. Sunil's pleading for forgiveness could be heard all over the hotel. Sunil threatened to end his life rather than face ignominy. He trembled thinking about the shame that would be the lot of his family and him.

When morning broke, they found Sunil swinging from the ceiling fan, another statistic in the gruelling life of the lone ranger. All bosses are not as blunt.

Jayashree Rajamani is a very demanding sales manager. A similar situation and accusation was confirmed by the internal audit. It was given to Jayashree to sack the team member, Subir. Sadly, he was also a star performer. She did not like being the executioner and decided not to take up the issue as it was late night and Subir was on tour. She would rather deal with it in the morning and not sully the dinner she was invited to. Unfortunately, someone from HO leaked the impending news to Subir.

Jayashree returned home late from the dinner to check her mobile, which she had left at home. There were 18 calls from Subir. Sensing that something had gone terribly wrong, she called up

Subir. It was an emotional and incoherent Subir who claimed that he was deeply regretful and begged another chance to repair his reputation. His mental state was at a breakdown. Jayashree quickly took things under control. She assured Subir that she would halt all efforts to sack him. She would review his case with HR and see if there was any way to change the decision. She asked Subir to wait until morning and see what could be done.

Jayashree knew that the panic of the night withers away with the bright rays of the morning sun. Early next morning, she called up Subir and was relieved when he answered the phone. She spoke to HR and requested a moratorium of 10 days before action be taken. By the ninth day, Subir had found an alternate employment and put in his resignation. Subir went on to do extremely well, having learnt a hard lesson. He rose to be a vice president sales of a small but aggressive company, in time. He never forgot the sensitivity Jayashree had shown him.

Keep bad news for the morning light and the rising sun. It beams hope.

19

Company Maketh the Man

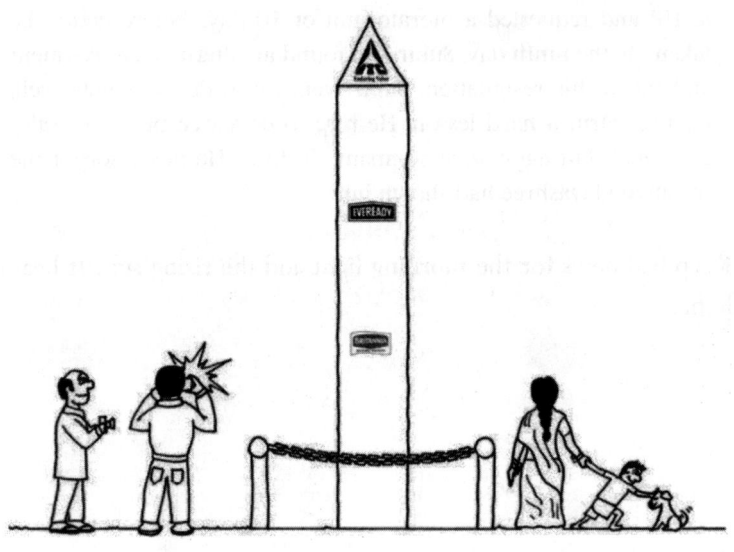

One of the joys of selling is the opportunity to meet a varied set of people. The trade, as they are clubbed together, are the warriors of the market. The wildlings from the popular 'Game of Thrones' could take notes from this happy bunch, who handle the movement of product into the interiors, far from the urban wholesale markets.

You see them all. The smart, the street savvy, the simple one, the cunning and the downright pirate, they are all there. As the salesperson trudges the markets, he has this motley crew for company. One can learn and unlearn all that was taught in graduate school.

Consider Babubhai, the scion of the formidable distribution firm K.D. Khemchand & Co. in Ahmedabad. They held all the prime agencies such as Levers, Eveready, Nestle and a fleet of other impressive brands. He had his brother operate with the similar range of brands in Pune. Both brothers were polished and very well educated. Babubhai would quote from the *Harvard Business Review* and look forward to meeting company salespeople who could hold a decent conversation.

Extremely wealthy and well travelled, Babubhai could size up visiting company personnel in a jiffy and know how to play them. He would sense the tension of the month's targets as he welcomed the visitor. He knew that the more troubled the salesperson, the greater the opportunity to buy with distress discounts. He also knew how the wholesale trade worked.

Even before the shipment from the company arrived, he had made deals that would involve shipping to the massive Masjid Bunder in Bombay. The differing tax rates between Gujarat and Maharashtra made a big difference, when they were evaded.

In between airing his views on the latest thinking on management, he would squeeze the company sales manager dry. Once he had entrapped them, it was impossible to untangle. Babubhai's favourite line was 'Every man has his price. My responsibility is to find out how much it is. After that, he cannot escape'.

Contrast Babubhai with the low-profile Nataraj Stores from Tirunelveli. One of the biggest distributors of South India.

Palliniswamy Nadar was the general manager who was the votive force. They had huge business interests, beyond distribution. They owned fireworks and match factories in Sivakasi. It was whispered that they were larger in turnover than many of the companies they were distributors for.

Palliniswamy and his team had a different view of the agency lines. They were grateful to the brands that started off Nataraj Stores. They even made plans to create a kind of monument to the founding brands such as ITC, Eveready, Britannia and other blue-chip companies. This was to be at the entrance to their head-quarters in Tirunelveli. Any visitor from the principal companies was treated with respect and accorded a reception that was austere but charming.

Gopal Chandra was the heavy weight distributor who had a peculiar interest. Gopal was a devotee of Guru Mahachandra, a local god—man who had a strong following. All priority was given to the working at the Guru Maha ashram. Especially on festive celebrations, the Ganapati worship was widely acclaimed. Gopal wore very conspicuously the prayer beads and the garland of the Rudraksh beads.

Gopal Chandra was quite different from everyday people one met. It was not until a couple of years later when someone noticed that Suburban Distributor's cheque had bounced, most uncharacteristically. Enquiries were made and there was no sign of Gopal or any of the residents of the ashram. When the dust settled, there was about ₹50,000,000 outstanding. Neither Gopal Chandra nor his Guru Maha was ever seen again.

Nagpur is considered quite the centre of India and had a certain mystery all of its own. It was the gateway to the Central Provinces and the trendsetter for many miles around. Moosan Ali was a distributor who was the doer. He understood that the opportunity lay in the pain of not meeting targets. He could sell anything, anywhere. That really was the problem. His throw was from a strong pitching arm. Stocks he bought could land up anywhere. It was rumoured that he was a whiz at handling sales managers.

Such salespeople saw little merit in keeping to the right side of the policies and found loopholes that were not above board. The salespeople dealing with such giants came away feeling inadequate. They became the role models for the easily impressionable. Company did make the man.

20

The Devil Made Me Do It

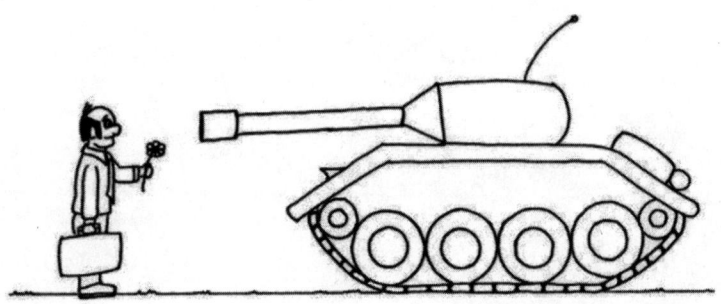

One consistent refrain of senior sales managers to the question 'Why do salespeople lie?' is that they have no choice. The boss made them do it. Is this really so?

Kuldeep Chavhan is today settled in Toronto and loves to remember the days he spent pushing pesticides to a blooming agri-market in India. Selling into the vast interiors of the subcontinent to illiterate farmers was a new experience for him. He had graduated from Pusa Institute, famed for its research and commitment to uplift the lot of the farmers. Kuldeep was snapped up by the multinational pesticides company that had set up a state-of-the-art factory in Bihar. He soon realized that even his bosses knew little about the field conditions.

Sales were patchy and in North India, they were extremely poor. Kuldeep could understand that the product launched had been wrong for the market. It did not impact the pests but was also three times more expensive than the leading brand used by the poor farmers. The head of the division was furious. All projections made to management had gone haywire. A hasty meeting was called to correct the looming failure.

The India head of the pesticide division was a Spaniard, Emilio Santos, whose accent, though quaint, was not easy to follow. Kuldeep felt it falling on him to speak the truth. Some of the teammates warned Kuldeep to keep his resignation handy as stating the truth was courageous but imprudent. Others who spoke before Kuldeep tried to support the product and claimed that more awareness could make the difference to the sales. He felt his throat getting parched at the thought of addressing the general manager of the division.

When it was given for Kuldeep to present, there was a silence in the room and the voice that he heard did not sound at all like him. He looked directly at Emilio and said in a grave voice, 'Our product is ineffective on use. It is three times more expensive. We should stop this cheating of poor farmers'.

There was a pin-drop silence while Emilio took stock. He stared at Kuldeep, speechless. Others in the meeting prepared for the typhoon. Nothing happened. Emilio bore his blue Spanish eyes deep into Kuldeep. He squinted and said clearly, for all to understand, 'Mr Chavhan, we are not highway robbers. If the product does not perform we will withdraw it, rework it and then try again'. Kuldeep looked at his teammates. They gave him a thumbs up. The reformulated pesticide was a great hit.

Ask any salesperson about lying and you get more stories of courage as examples of running against the wind. Yet, how does one explain how instances of gross malpractice happen? It had happened to Anita.

Straight from doing her MBA, Anita was put through the induction programme and as part of the toughening process asked to handle a sales territory that was vacated by a salesperson who had resigned to get a job as a regional head. The company was in the business of selling batteries for torches and transistor radios. 'C' size batteries were a dropping demand as there were few equipment that used 'C' size.

She visited the distributor's shop to the chant of the woes that had been caused by the previous incumbent. Anita decided to make a physical count of the stocks. To her horror, she found 95 cases of 'C' batteries. Off-take in the previous year was just two cases. To add to the situation, the expiry date was just a month away.

She called the office and was told that nothing could be done as the distributor bought it knowing the slow movement of the product. Anita contacted some big wholesalers and made a distress sale. The product moved but surely was consumed by a consumer who was unable to read the date of expiry.

Kuldeep, now older and wiser, has this insight to share.

The majority of those who join sales come from deprived backgrounds. Most do not choose to be salespeople. It was the only job they could get. To lie and keep the job is easy when there is no alternative. Often, they are in dread of their bosses who have realized that they have no other job offers. It becomes the tyranny of the bonded labour, well nearly so.

21

When All Hell Breaks Loose

Sales closing is one of the most toxic of all times. The good, bad and ugly all pounce to make the month closing even more unbelievable than an Italian spaghetti western.

This is the time of the month when rising decibel attempts to compensate for dropping sales. Or so it is hoped. All the best and worst in sales management is on exhibition. The urgency of the last few days of invoicing is poignant in this story from the times when all phones were through the exchange and the call was relayed from one exchange to another. If a call was made from Bombay to Jabalpur, it would first be directed to Nagpur and then on to Jabalpur.

This was the last day of month-closing and every distributor was being tapped for whatever extra could be invoiced against a demand draft, something like a banker's cheque. The sales officer from Bombay was shouting loudly enough to be heard in Jabalpur without the aid of the phone, 'Please make an urgent payment of ₹50,000 before close of banking hours so that we can ship you some extra stocks'. The distributor in Jabalpur kept pleading that he was unable to hear the message, as the phone call was indistinct.

The long-distance operator in Nagpur who was assisting in the call could hear both parties, Bombay and Jabalpur, very distinctly. She decided to help and spoke to the Jabalpur distributor, repeating verbatim what the sales officer from Bombay was trying to communicate. On hearing this, the distributor told the operator, 'Miss I can't hear anything. If you can hear them, why don't you send them the ₹50,000 yourself?'

Month-ending at other times can be exhilarating. It was monsoon time and it was an added challenge. Mumbai was slowing down and the traffic was a pitiable crawl. It took four hours to reach Fort from Santa Cruz. Yet the spirit of Mumbai is amazing. People find their way by any mode of transport. They climb on to trucks when the suburban railway stops.

By mid-day, there were only three territories that reported in and it looked that the month would be a bomb. Yet, one by one, each salesperson waded through knee-deep water to bring in orders. There was no sign of Jaokar who manned the highly potential Solapur/Kolhapur sales territory. It was not the age of the mobile phone. As hope withered, suddenly there was a cheer as Jaokar squelched through the doors with a broad smile on his face and not a dry patch of cloth on his body.

There was a short fall from the target and all assembled sales team did their best to add on. By the end of a very wet day, the sun came shining through. With the sunshine came the hope. The branch had beaten the target. That joy is a special experience. Sales teams deserve to have such moments. They really bond as one unit at such moments.

Fortune favours the brave and bold they say. One can also add the foolish. It was one of those poor years of the economy, and the sale of flashlights was running way below plan. The marketing team felt that a contest for sales teams could lift the fortunes. However, as the year dragged by, hardly any of the branches seemed destined to win the cash prizes that were meant for the winning teams.

The general sales manager looked at the branches most likely to stand a chance. Guwahati branch was asked to try and make the prize. The branch was led by a young sales manager who had a great sales team, each one truly engaged in making the targets. The average sales of flashlights in Guwahati for a month were about 40,000 torches. To make the year-end figure, it meant selling about 120,000 flashlights in December.

The power of a fully engaged sales team is visible in what they managed to pull off for the month: 165,000 pieces, an all-time high. This, of course, meant that January sales were next to nothing. There were a few returns even in February from overloading. Things looked bleak for the first quarter sales as each stockist point was filled to the brim. Sometimes there is divine intervention when the intentions are noble.

The flashlight plant had major labour problems in March and stayed closed for three months. Product went short in wholesale markets, and the market rates went up to include a premium. Only Guwahati branch had adequate stocks. The trade celebrated with sales at profitable margins.

Heaven helps those who try and don't give up hope.

22

For Whom the Bell Tolls

As written earlier, the closest similarity to the lifestyle of the sales world is probably the army. The pressure to perform and achieve is immense. In a Gallup poll, it was determined that 35 per cent of all salespeople are misfits for the job. Only about 20 per cent are engaged in their jobs.

It sometimes happens that the pressure is more than can be borne. *The New York Times* sent a team to India to investigate. A report was published on 11 August 2016. It captures the tough environment of sales, especially in pharmaceutical sales.

Talbot Laboratories, India (name changed), is the second largest pharma company in India. One of their top salespeople in Indore, Anil Sharma, unable to deal with the pressure of meeting targets, leaving his wife and two children at home, rode his motorcycle to a lonely stretch of railroad and jumped in front of a speeding train. His body was identified the next day.

In his pocket was a note that said, 'I am going to commit suicide because I can't meet my company's sales targets and my company is pressurizing me'. In sympathy, more than 250 sales team members walked off the job for a day of solidarity. The union of MRs called for new rules to moderate sales practices and bring some sanity to the mad wild world of pharma selling. It might not save another casualty.

It seems Talbot Labs had a sales development activity called 'health camps'. These were set up to drum up business for the doctors who in turn would prescribe Talbot Lab drugs. The testing at the health camps was done by the sales team who were not licensed to do it.

As the battle of the giants in medicine grows more bloody, the collateral damage are the Anil Sharmas of this world. The report speaks of how Anil did well in the company and allowed his little family the joys of buying a car and even managed to buy an apartment. He was feted as one of the performing sales stars. The idyllic situation gave way to money worries, and the bonuses were not coming easy.

A change of bosses made it harder as newer and higher demands on sales were being made. Anil's rapport with his new boss was on the wane. He feared a transfer from Indore to Chennai. This is standard process when a salesperson is being asked to go. Anil panicked. It was Sunday and he feared the next day he would be asked to quit. He abandoned life instead.

It is possible to examine the many reasons for such a sad event. In the end, there is a clammy feeling of knowing there is no recourse. What had to happen did just happen.

Patient Screening had the logic of it being a community service. The company had targets to be met even for the health camps. The industry had little concern for following the rules of ethical selling. In fact, it was expected that to go the extra mile required breaking industry rules. If one is not a 'sissy', one just had to do what must be done to ensure the sales. Each month it got harder.

There are instances when to help meet the targets, sales reps have spent their own money to incentivize the doctors. This kind of desperation to sell is not an exception. More industries appear to be caught in the sway. As these companies are better paymasters than the industry norm, quitting does not come as an easy step to take.

While the urge to end it all appeals to those who are at breaking point, there are others who depend on a good round of drinking, to get drunk. After a while, this becomes a daily need and a time comes when it becomes the highlight of the day and the nights recede. The liver is the first organ to give way. Once that starts, there is a domino effect and many organs give up the fight. So many stalwarts have gone down, unsung.

It is a staggering realization that fatalities can happen. Ashok was a brilliant engineer and excellent in industrial sales. He was a really affable man and a loving, family man. At one annual sales conference in Bangalore (now Bengaluru), when everyone was busy with activities, Ashok's liver gave up the uneven fight. He was rushed home and never made it.

To the Ashoks and Anils of this sales world, a tribute of acknowledgement: Yes, it is a tough and unfair world, you tried to deal with it as best as you could. Rest easy, mates. No more targets to make.

23

Either You Don't Know, or You Are Lying

Sales chiefs have a significant impact on the culture of the sales organization. Some are true leaders and make it their responsibility to develop their team, especially those directly reporting to them. Others spread a sense of fear and trepidation. After the party is over, there is always the assessment of even the smallest player to consign to history the net worth of the man. History written by the people is rarely wrong.

Sandeep Choudhuri typified the hard-drinking, hard-working, fire-spitting and ruthless sales head every sales team member loved to hate. He was young and seemed to have been given a license to freeze by management. Most of those, subject to his scorn and abusive language, would clam up and be frozen with terror.

Sandeep could keep touring relentlessly and nothing appeared to fatigue him. The chain-smoking and rivulets of whisky, as the sun set, would charge him up with energy. He had his favourites, and they did his bidding with no questions asked. This select group could get away with any atrocity. No one dared to tell on them.

It happened when Sandeep realized that one of the sales branch managers Venkie had greater clout than Sandeep imagined. Sandeep had to suffer the ignominy of watching Venkie openly challenge his authority. This manager took all the risk. He died of a sudden heart attack while at a sales conference at the HO. It was a shock when his body was flown back to his shattered widow.

Venkie was a hard-working salesperson, to the point that his widow felt he had neglected his family and all else to meet his targets for the company. In her anguish, the widow expressed her heartbreak by wishing that she could have buried her husband with a brass flashlight in place of a cross. Sandeep felt that in dying, Venkie had played the most effective card. He could never be criticized.

Sandeep, as all-India sales manager, came to take charge of the branch. His scorn for the sales officers who reported to Venkie was difficult to hide. He asked the four of them to report to his room in Hotel Grand at Churchgate at about 6 in the evening. He sat and spat insults on the dead Venkie and ridiculed the team for not being more assertive. He kept calling for whisky after whisky and finally let off the team at 1:30 AM, without a morsel of food. He repeated this for three evenings in a row. Perhaps he was purging Venkie from the branch.

Others are smoother. Gajinder Solankie was an important head of the consumer products distribution company. Their products were varied, including baby products, shaving accessories and cell phones.

Gajinder was a cool operator. He had some strong beliefs. Like he always told the truth and all else were liars. His favourite insight was that there are two kinds of salespeople. The first are those who don't know the facts and tell you nothing worthwhile, even if they are telling the truth. He preferred the second type: they know the truth and choose to lie. Gajinder felt that a person who is not aware of the real situation is not worth anything.

Gajinder was wily as a fox. He kept himself well informed and always did his sales strategy with the least of fanfare. He realized that the wholesale movement of a product seals its fate. He made sure that the best deals were saved for the big product movement. He was protective of his team and would go to any extent to defend them publicly. Thereafter, he would strip the hapless salesperson of all dignity and, at times, the job.

Through it all, he held the moral high ground and would incessantly lecture on the virtues of working to a system. He conspired to damage his competition with what he called the seamless knife. This is the knife whose cut is so fine that there is little to show for the cut. It still appears to be a thrust with no blood split.

As is wont with these types of leaders, the objective is to be ahead of everyone and hold a position of integrity, all this while doing what must be done to achieve the goals, with no real scruples.

Both the types create an atmosphere of uncertainty and distrust. This does not develop people to be confident. They cling to anything to keep their jobs, lies and whatever else.

24

Tainted by the Company One Keeps

Venkie, who has been mentioned in the previous chapter, was the incorrigible salesperson. If you recall, it was his wife who wanted to place a flashlight on his grave instead of a cross. There was a manic obsession that ruled all that Venkie did. He went on tours without a plan.

He would suddenly decide that his presence was required in Surat. Without packing a toothbrush, he would take a taxi to the airport, buy a ticket and surprise the distributor there. He would then give the list of toiletries and innerwear to be purchased.

The story of Venkie's ad hoc travels became sales legend. The stories, told and retold, ended up sounding like this: Venkie, they said, would decide on impulse to go on a tour. He would reach the Santa Cruz airport and take the first flight that was leaving for any of the cities in his sales zone. If he was hoping to go to Surat and found that there was an earlier flight to Ahmedabad, he would board the flight for Ahmedabad.

At a quarterly sales meet, a branch manager of a neighbouring branch publicly chastised Venkie for cross-state sales. He was embarrassed and had really not organized any such sale. An angry Venkie called up from Calcutta itself and ordered his sales officer to send two truckloads of batteries to Hyderabad, the erring branch. When the Hyderabad branch manager landed in his city, he was greeted by the news that six trucks of batteries had landed from Bombay.

Venkie was at his naughty best when faced with the prospect of year-ending sales. He knew nothing would come in the way of his targets. As December drew to a close, he had many problems beyond the orders. As branches dug in to save the year-end figures, there was a shortage of the red battery. Bombay city would take no other colour but red.

The only batteries still with the branch godown were white batteries. The earliest Bombay could hope for was after year-end sales. To top it all, internal audit swooped down on the branch to ensure the fairness of the depot closing. Hawk-eyes watched as every carton of batteries were under scrutiny. Venkie realized that with no red batteries, he would fall short of his commitment to HO. He ordered that the Bombay distributors be invoiced the unsaleable white batteries. He promised to replace them with red ones as soon as the truck reached. The trade refused to accept the wrong batteries. So, they were invoiced to them and kept aside in the company godown.

Internal audit got wind of the scheme and decided to pay a surprise raid on the company godown in Thane. Venkie heard of their plan at about 7:30 in the evening. He sent his team to hire a temporary godown and before daylight he had shifted all the white batteries he had invoiced to the Bombay trade. By the time the audit team reached Thane the following morning, not a piece of the offending battery was present.

These were the stalwarts of an era who stuck their neck out to protect their word. In doing so, they sent a message that no rule was sacred when the 'number' was at stake. They put themselves at risk and the company at even a larger one in terms of governance and the law. They worked selflessly and neglected their families. They were also buried without a torch on their headstone.

SB was another of the kind. He was senior in the Calcutta branch and quite fancied himself fit for Tollywood, the filmdom of Calcutta. Each act of sales was an act he felt capable of stealing the show. He was chosen to take the management trainee on tour and show how sales were achieved. He chose to demonstrate how an order was to be booked. The young trainee, still wet in the gills, was the sole audience to the show enacted at SB's hotel room.

Amarnath was the Darjeeling distributor's eldest son and not as savvy as his father. SB was all dressed in a light sweater as nights could be quite cold in the pretty hill station. He had invited Amarnath to have a drink and dinner after. He prominently displayed an unopened bottle of White Knight whisky, the best from the Meakins brewery.

As Amarnath came in, he warmly greeted him and poured out a double peg of the golden liquid. Amarnath looked very excited and scared. His father did not know of his awe for the White Knight. SB brushed aside his feeble protests and poured himself a small peg. As the whisky took hold, SB changed tack.

He asked why the monthly reports were late in coming and for the following 45 minutes literally started to mercilessly berate him. Short of profanity, he used all kinds of toxic words to show his displeasure. Each time this happened, poor Amarnath gulped on his White Knight for fortitude. SB skilfully reloaded his drink and soon the White Knight looked in need of reinforcement. SB stuck to nursing his first drink.

As Amarnath grew unsteady, SB changed the topic to the month's order booking. Amarnath now was emboldened to say that he had enough stocks to last a long lifetime. This seemed to burst a blood vessel in SB. He raised his voice and roared, 'You can go to hell. I will appoint another distributor in Darjeeling'. Amarnath realized that his jaunty retort was ill received. He apologized profusely and asked that 'Saheb' to please write out the order and he blindly signed it.

SB looked at the wildered trainee and winked. When Amarnath left, rather wobbly, SB turned to his audience of one and asked, 'So how was I?'

The audience of one cheered lustily.

25

Sales Malpractice

Medical professionals across the world have sleepless nights thinking about the possibility of malpractice suits. Patients who consider the line of treatment to be faulty or negligent are increasingly suing for millions of dollars. Courts are partial to considering the damage sustained by patients and award them large amounts of money in compensation payment.

In 1994, McDonald's, the burger giant, got sued by a customer who was scalded by the coffee that was spilt from the coffee cup and onto the lady who was balancing the hot cup between her thighs. The New Mexico civil jury awarded $2.86 million to plaintiff Stella Liebeck. Eventually, after appeals by McDonald's, she was paid $640,000. Now the coffee cups come with safety warnings.

Why is there a growing trend in people suing companies and one another? There are, of course, pliant lawyers who are willing to fight such cases for a percentage of the awards they can win. However, it is much more than that. Consumers spoilt for choice feel entitled to flawless service and satisfaction from the product or service they have paid for. Anything less than their expectation is deemed a breach of contract.

Even the legal profession gets sued, as do architects builders and other service providers. Can the writing be on the wall for the salespeople too? How long before the scrutiny turns to the actions of the sales group? You don't read about salespeople being sued for wrong selling, though there are numerous instances of this malady. Companies, across the globe, are seriously considering leaning on this option. Each year, companies write off millions of dollars and try to cover up the incidents caused by their sales personnel. Shareholders don't look kindly on such losses.

Perhaps, one of the reasons for this could be the lack of standards or operating protocol in a sales process. There is nobody that defines what is right and wrong in sales. All that is important is whether the sale was made.

Companies are grappling with the issues of corporate governance, especially after the Wall Street crash of 2008. The recession that followed was in part because of the flaunting of all safety norms in the real estate deals.

'Sales malpractice' is a new word in the sales lexicon. Companies are asking questions about high return of products after invoicing, expired goods and poor service claims. Someone has to be held accountable. If goods have been sold in excess of demand, what is the role of the salesperson to ensure that the velocity of money is not hampered?

At times, customer-centric policies provide the opportunity for wrong selling. Consider the policy of replacing time-expired products. This is done to ensure goods of the highest quality reach the customer. It also provided the opportunity to load an outlet mercilessly. Salespeople realize that whatever is excess will return back to the company. A large distribution company found that their returns were as high as 7 per cent of their sales. This had a crushing impact on their profitability. They took a drastic decision to announce a 'no-return policy'. Their sales continued to grow but their returns dropped. This went straight to the bottom line.

The difference was that now the responsibility of the salesperson shifted from mere ensuring sales numbers to managing age of stocks. This too is a part of good selling process. Customers who first objected to the change in policy saw, in time, great benefit as they were certain that the age of stocks was also being monitored by the selling company. This saved a lot of paperwork that involves credit notes and unending follow-up. It saved their time and the hassle.

So what is a sales malpractice really? Here is the definition of a malpractice:

> The breach by a member of a profession of either a standard of care or a standard of conduct. Malpractice refers to negligence or

misconduct by a professional person such as a lawyer, a doctor, a dentist or an accountant. (19th National Congress of CPC)

Put in the sales context, malpractice has been defined by the senior sales vice-president of an international bank very clearly: 'Sales Malpractice is when a customer has been sold one dollar more than the real need. You have then committed Sales Malpractice'.

This is a chilling call to understand the nature of the sales process. Salespeople are justified by the service they do for the customer. They help to make better buying decisions. However, if, by manipulation, they effect sales that damage the interest of the customer, it is negligent behaviour by the salesperson.

It is then a criminal act.

26

A Sales System, Really?

When Jack Carew, who founded the Carew Positional Selling System, first joined sales as a rep, he discovered that no one followed a sales system. He even did a study to locate what was common among salespeople. Everyone seemed focused on the sales results. Fast talking and glib ways were what was considered to win sales. Very little about the customer, everything was about closing the order.

In fact, there was serious discussion about how unnecessary it was. All that was required was good product knowledge and persuading the customer by any available means. He was ridiculed for trying to establish a system. There was also little understanding of the role a salesperson played, except to earn a commission.

The ingress of recruits into this line of work was also a tad questionable. Those who had no other choice of career looked at this emerging field of work. There were no lofty notions of the service provided. It was merely to get an unwilling consumer to agree to buy a product or service.

The image of the salesperson as a high-energy, hard-to-evade person grew, and with it started a reluctance to trust the easy promises made. A system has with it a certain accountability that allows a trail. That was not always a good thing and soon sales teams came up with a collective and individual-based aversion to writing reports. This is an international phenomenon.

Anita had a very pleasing sales presence and also a very attractive personality. She could charm any customer with her smile and elegant banter. Every month-end, the sales branch depended on Anita to do more than her quota, and she did it graciously. She was extremely popular with her teammates, except with her boss for just one thing. She would not fill any of the daily reports. Even her expense reports were behind, with money due to her.

One day Anita left the job for a really dreamy one. She found herself with a team of young salespeople. They looked up to her for direction. Anita, in her new avatar, insisted that all the reports she never got down to filling be regularly filled by her team. Today, she is the chairman of a multinational freight-forwarding company, and her responsibilities are for the whole Asia–Pacific region. Anita today has only reports to surround her. That is how she controls the whole region. She now swears by reports.

Adil has just graduated out of an MBA school and finds that the company he joined insisted that all marketing trainees have to spend a year as front-line salespeople. Nothing he learned at graduation school prepared him for the chaos he found. He was asked to shadow a senior salesperson Sudesh, who treated him as a curiosity. He felt that Adil was too young to know the complications of the market, yet he was impressed that Adil was a graduate of a top-rung business college.

Except for introducing him to all the trade, there was precious little that Adil could understand about selling. All the moves made by Sudesh seemed based on previous relationships, cast over many years. Adil was not given a chance to sell, only to observe.

Adil was asked to control a medium-sized sales territory. He found that all that the trade spoke about was of the tough times that were being experienced. At the end of the first month, he was way below the target. Sudesh tried to console him. Adil suspected that his MBA was no longer held in great esteem. After all, what do universities know about a real market? Sudesh assured Adil that in time he would pick up and do fine. Adil wondered if the company would even confirm him.

Ramdas is a vice-president sales of a big distribution company in Qatar. He leads the sales team, comprised of all expat Indians. The difficult visa rules make it hard to send back sales team members who are not performing. Assured of a nearly permanent job, quite a few give priority to personal commitments, rather than work. He works late into the night, trying to give direction, signing daily reports, and tries to sort out the personality issues that dog all such operations.

At times, Ramdas wonders if coming so far from home was at all worth it. He wishes that there could be a way to get all his team follow a system of selling. He tried to instil order and found that nobody cared to follow it.

Is it at all possible to bring system to a sales force, he wondered.

27

The Power of Discipline

All expats who make a living, being far from home, both enjoy their experience of living in strange lands and rue it. Mark Tully, the famous writer and journalist, has become so much a part of the Indian scene that often people around him have to be reminded that he is no local lad. Living away from home makes finding the way back home rather a challenge. Especially, this is true for those expats living in Asia.

Asia has no real common theme running through. Rules change as the borders change. Even the racial mix is complex. The sight of the expat in one of the many watering holes of the main cities is a reassuring sign. *Time* magazine reported that one such correspondent retired from her assignment in Vietnam and planned to enjoy being in the USA again, but for good. That is when she was struck by the definite lack of freedom in the USA!

The 'Land of the Free', as the USA is called, has the largest number of rules that impact every aspect of living in the country. Asia, in contrast, has fewer rules and even fewer people who follow them.

Even in a metropolis, such as Mumbai, there is a strange convention of ignoring the traffic lights after 10 at night. Cars shoot through red lights with gay abandon, and it is said that shooting a red light at night is the safer way to drive as every driver does it with watchful eyes. If you really assume that driving confidently through a green light is safe driving, you could well be hit by someone speeding through a red light.

It is said that to maintain its unenviable record of freedom, the USA has to enforce a multitude of rules so that no one impinges on the freedom of the other. Many Asian countries are far from free, but their citizens do pretty much what they like, though their constitutional rights may be missing in parts. The sales world is very Asian in this sense.

Sales managers are great at urging their teams to push that little harder and not to miss any chance to sell more. It is quite akin to a

Ferrari with no brakes. Month-ending is full of surprises and shocks. To balance the shocks, decisions are taken that can at a calmer moment be considered unwise and perhaps downright foolish. It is important to set very clear rules. How to sell, when to sell and when to stop selling are necessary to establish. Rules may appear as being too constrictive, but to really enjoy the freedom and joy of selling, it is recommended that a clear-cut sales system is enforced.

What is not clear to most sales teams is that the real purpose of a sale is to see that the product, or service, is consumed within a relatively short space of time. Companies that sell goods that have a 'Use Before' clause are the most to be hit by sloppy selling. All goods returned are a loss. It matters little that who bears the loss. It is wasteful and reflects a poor understanding of the role of the salesperson in avoiding this expense.

When sales managers ignore the tenets of responsible selling, they are complicit in the act of sales malpractice. That sets in motion a damaging collusion between levels of management. This eventually douches the fire of management leadership. Bad selling, finally, is a crumbling of leadership. Efforts to cover up the mess further aggravates things. When things go out of hand, the only recourse is a change in leadership.

It is unfair to the sales team. They are never able to feel that a job is well done. Every monster sales month-ending has its share of headaches and issues regarding credit, payment delays and sadly bad debts. It is time to let the team know that good selling is appreciated and bad selling is a malpractice not supported by management.

28

What's Worth Doing
Is Worth Doing Well

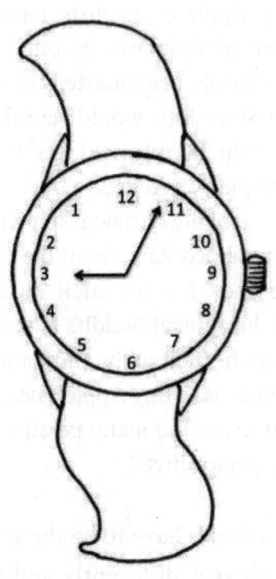

Simon Sinek, the world famous author of the quote 'People don't buy what you sell, they buy why you sell...', raised the question in his now famous Ted.com speech that great companies do things differently.

They don't talk about the features and benefits of their product, or how they do what they do; they appeal straight to the fuzzy part of the brain that controls all decision-making. He goes on to talk of why Apple is an admired company. They don't speak of what the product does but why they do what they do.

> Over the years, Apple has had, across the world, individuals who were considered the Apple evangelists. Ram Ray, the advertising wizard and founder of Response, is one such. Over 20 years ago, he would fly to Apple headquarters in Cupertino, California, to be present when Steve Jobs would reveal the new products of Apple. On one such trip, he returned to Calcutta with a gift from Apple, given to all Apple evangelists.
>
> It was an ordinary-looking chronograph wrist watch, powered by a battery. His friends ribbed Ram about the cheap Japanese watch. Hardly worthwhile they felt for such an advanced technology company. Ram with his typical Buddha look asked them to observe the hands of the watch. Incredibly, the hands of the watch were moving anti-clockwise, asserting Apple's belief that life can be a lot different if we want to see the many possibilities. Why not see the world from another perspective?

Why does the world of sales have to be the same old uncanny thing? Is there a way to look at it differently and transform it with also improving its productivity?

If I have to lie to sell more, how great would it be if, by telling only the truth, we sold even more? Or is it only a fantasy? Is the real world unable to prosper on the truth?

Nothing changes by only dreaming it. Every dream has to be followed up by back-breaking effort to implement the change.

To resolve to tell the truth appears to be a moralistic view. Truth is not an effort. Not to tell the truth is far more taxing. Every lie has to be remembered and covered up. It has to be ensured that there is no trail after.

Telling the truth has to be a default system. It can only be so if there is a robust system to back up the sales activities. This is where a professional sales system has to be the foundation of all sales work. No system can work without the buy-in of not only the top sales management but also the CEO of the organization.

Every system can produce results that it is designed for. At times, the needs of a month, or the uncontrollable external variables, may negatively impact the results. Here is where the top management has to accept that tampering with the system is contra-productive and fraught with sorry consequences, both in the short run and more in the long. Only this can give the salesperson the confidence to believe that what has been done is optimal under the circumstances. It also has the support of the line bosses.

Across the world, there is a school of thought that asserts that in sales, one only needs to ask and more orders magically appear. Sales managers have taught themselves to never say never, or that enough is really enough. Mindless application of the pressure theory of sales has resulted in a constant feeling of being inadequate. This weighs on the salesperson and wrecks the little build-up of self-assurance. Telling lies, then, appears to be a low-risk option, until one can find a more suitable job.

If we take Sinek's question, and to apply to a selling, it can be asked, why does one choose a selling career? Often when posed this question, the answer is a simple one word, 'money'. Very few see any lofty ideals to follow. Perhaps, therein lie some of our problems. Are salespeople mere mercenaries?

Why do we do what we do? What really happens to those salespeople who don't know why? Worse still, what happens to their customers? There is a need to believe in a system of selling and stick with it.

29
Freedom from Avoidable Worry

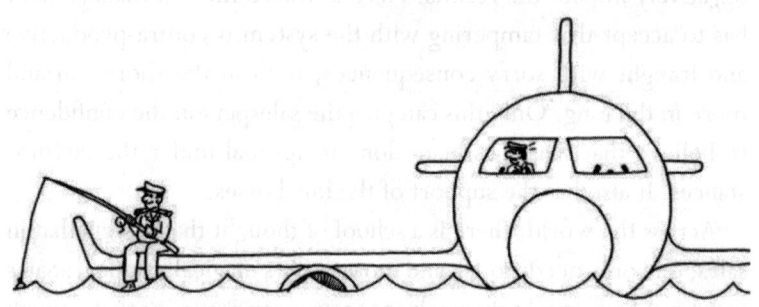

Worry is the irritating sense of foreboding doom, caused by fear. Unfortunately, there are a number of fears simultaneously being dealt within a person's brain. Worry signals that emanate from fear have a nagging quality that tends to blend rather than stay separate.

In her work, Katherine Schafler, NYC-based psychologist, suggests that worry is a way of avoiding the fear that wells up in everyone. Worry is to avoid feeling the fear. It is in a way a dodge that avoids confronting fear. It really does nothing to solve the source of the fear, but rather adds to the overall sense of unease. All worries working in tandem cause the epidemics of the modern day: stress.

Schafler goes on to say that there is a positive to handling fear—possibility of growth for the individual. However, worry is rewarded with more worry. If one addresses the source of worry, which is fear, the worries will melt away.

The human being is still alive and prospering, thanks in part to the nature of fear. It asked that there be caution exercised at most times as cave people were subject to predators. Although the modern times have none of the constant fears of predators, there is still a growing number of urban fears that have to be reviewed for relevance.

People do not live on trees any more, when the fears are justified. While there could have been a great reduction in the number of fears, modern living has only increased the numbers. Mental health has suffered as a result and the drug companies do good business with medicines that tackle depression. Salespeople are high net worth customers for this industry.

There are a number of high-stress vocations. The airline pilot performs a feat each time the flight takes off that defies nature. Yet they don't seem to have the need to balance their lives with a quota of lies.

The surgeon, the ship captain, the astronaut, the circus trapeze artists, the Formula 1 drivers and just so many other careers have even a greater fear factor than the humble sales line. Yet they seem to manage their job stress within control.

There seems to be a connecting link between all these careers— robust training and a clarity about what is the goal and a laid-out pattern of how to get there. There is little room for error and when a commercial airline takes off or lands, there is a strict checklist of what is to be done in every situation the plane may face.

When Captain Sully of the Hudson River landing fame was quizzed about his instant decision to land the crippled aircraft into the icy waters of the Hudson River, he had to defend his actions based on the standard operating procedure. He saved the lives of over 150 people and crew by keeping his fears in check by applying years of training in the air force and commercial flying. It does appear that while fears are not avoidable, these can also be channelled to developing a better and more skilful individual.

Sales fears are part of the package. It gets accentuated when sales teams operate in murky waters and do not understand their role in getting in their sales results. They are quizzed only on why their numbers were not met. They are told that they have to, come what may, achieve the sales commitments. There is no effort to indicate how that should be done. This increases the worry, and motivation of the team comes crashing down.

Team motivation is a topic that needs little introduction. Truckloads of theory has been written on the subject. Yet there is little clarity. On the ground and running, how does one deal with initiating, maintaining and growing the confidence of the team? How much does fear and worry erode this nebulous asset?

The Indian cricket team is a case in point. The surprise World Cup win in 1983 changed the future of the game in India. There came about an understanding that being world champions can be more than a flash in the pan. Money came in, along with fitness, international coaches and more than anything else, a professional attitude to the game fostered by great captains and superstars of the game. Today, the Indian team is a well-oiled machine that works with discipline and has a system that is the winning formula. Today, it is hard to imagine a poor show from the team (not that it never happens) as they are truly professional and world-class.

Being professional is the way to go.

30
Motivation: A Bath Needed Daily

Zig Ziglar was one of the greatest motivational speakers and a pro-lific author. He is no more but continues to inspire generations of his fans. A story about him goes like this. He had just concluded a meeting and a lady came up to register her disappointment. It appears that Zig had been a speaker at her company, and she found that the motivational level had dropped after a few days. She looked at Zig for an explanation.

Zig laughed his special laugh and told the lady, 'People often say that motivation does not last. Well, neither does bathing—that's why we recommend it daily'.

Many managers worry that they are not able to motivate their teams well enough and that explains the poor results. There is even a common belief that employees don't leave an organization; they leave bad bosses. This really gets bosses worried. They would not like the exiting employee to state that they were the reason for quit-ting. HR department takes immediate note of such proclamations and soon everyone points to the 'bad boss'.

In today's fast-moving world, there is less time to consider why a person is not motivated. If it does not impact the sales results, the level of motivation is not an issue. If it does, then it is a bit of a bother. Most bosses ask a statutory 'Is everything alright?' Some don't even wait to hear the response.

Yet, engaged employees make all the difference. It is the single greatest multiplier of sales performance. A Gallup poll of 2002 spoke of an alarming fact: seventy-five per cent of the sales force are not engaged in the work they do. They do maintenance work to just hold on to the job. The same survey had another disconcerting finding: thirty-five per cent of salespeople do not belong in sales.

Motivational theories are plentiful, for instance, the theory based on the Hawthorne Effect studies employee productivity done in the 1920s. The experiments took place in Hawthorne, a suburb of Chicago, at Western Electric's factory. It was conducted for the main part by Elton Mayo, an Australia-born sociologist. The experiment tried to check worker productivity under various lighting conditions. When the lights were increased, the productivity went up. Interestingly enough, even when the lights were dimmed, the productivity went up.

It was concluded that physical conditions were not changing the productivity, but the fact that they were being studied and someone cared.

In 1959, Herzberg propounded the two-factor theory: hygiene and dual factor. Workers are motivated by job enlargement, enrichment and empowerment. Factors such as pay, clean working conditions and positive relations with colleagues are perquisites to working. Their presence does not make for serious motivation.

A lot of attention has been given to creating events for employees that give them variety from the monotony of work. Their absence can cause some demotivation, especially if there is a history of such activities. Today, the understanding of motivation is a little different. As much as one strives to motivate a salesperson, the individual must choose to be motivated. The company can provide the conditions for a person to self-motivate. However, after that, the old adage 'You can take a horse to water, but you cannot make it drink' applies.

Providing the conditions for a salesperson to be motivated is an area for consideration. Most salespeople travel frequently out of the sales office. Their travel and conditions of accommodation can be hygiene factors. Most sales jobs are well regulated and do not continuously provide opportunity for job enlargement, enrichment or empowerment. So where does the motivating factor come into play?

It has been seen that sales teams that are left unsupervised with little heed paid to their development have major issues concerning motivation. The more the team has clear guidelines for working and are coached to perform better, the greater the apparent motivation and willingness among them to be engaged in their jobs.

Increasingly today, there are cautions that are reflected in a lesser threshold for failure. Turnover of sales staff is a chronic problem. Many run from companies that are unable to succeed in the market. Start-ups have a greater challenge getting good sales personnel for just this reason.

Having a professional sales system strengthens the organization and slows down the loss of salespeople to other companies. This itself is a cementing factor. For every salesperson that leaves, there are more who remain and start having doubts and looking for another job. When there is a steady sales team, with few departures, there is a condition for motivation. Sales teams are engaged.

31
Principles of Professional Selling

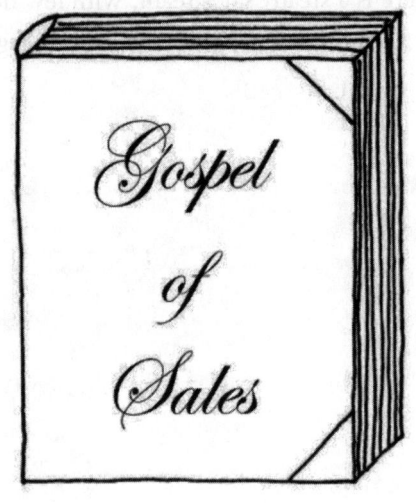

There are some who believe that the sales area is a field that defies all principles. The only thing that works is a hyped-up sense of commitment and pragmatic moves to corner the order. Meeting the target is the sacred goal. Everything else is as the situation warrants it.

Yet across the world, there is a move to define some irrefutable truths about selling that will stand the test of time. Every salesperson must decide whether to sell ethically, not because of the moral viewpoint, but rather the sales logic it makes. It is a researched fact that salespeople who define their values are trusted more and can sell more. So, the first principle of professional selling is to have the 'Code of the Salesperson'.

This code starts with the five fundamentals of ethical selling:

1. Integrity
2. Objectivity about customers' needs
3. Professional competence
4. Caring thoughtfulness to benefit the customer
5. Professional behaviour, at all times, especially on losing an order

Brian Tracy, one of the sales gurus, has the concept of the Golden Rule. Brian says that one should sell to other people the way they would like to be sold to. 'Do unto others as you would have them do unto you'. He literally recommends that you should 'Love thy neighbour as yourself'. This appears to not make business sense. However, in an infinite game, as Simon Sinek likes to view business, it does make money sense.

The following are some abiding principles of selling:

1. Always be selling to a person, not the organization. This is an important principle, even if one is selling to NASA. There is a person who will decide. All learning related to what helps dealing with a person will be applicable.

2. All selling must start with creating a positive impression. There is a stage of selling oneself before the product or service can be considered.
3. Always be asking questions to trap the gap of the customer. The needs define the solution and not the other way around.
4. Listening to understand is a far more useful talent than just listening to reply. Sales too are impacted positively.
5. Solutions to the gap of the customer must only be limited to the features that directly meet identified customer needs. If a need cannot be identified, there is no logic for pushing a sale.
6. Sell based on value created, not the price. Haggling may be a convention, but the sale is really based on accurately fulfilling the customer's needs.
7. 'Itching to pitch' is only after the needs are established and the solution based on the benefit to the customer is designed. Most salespeople go straight to pitching, skipping the stages of need identification or building a solution.
8. Be professional at all times. This means use of parliamentary language, holding back emotions that indicate frustration and always be willing to be of service again.
9. Be credible, at all costs. This is the fuel on which relationships grow.
10. Know why you are in the business of sales. If you are not sure, then change jobs.

David Mattson, CEO of the well-regarded Sandler Training, highlights some of the principles salespeople get wrong, some of the time.

Salespeople make an assumption that the customer is fully aware of all the needs. Very often, the expert salesperson is able to diagnose the real problem of the customer and is able to provide a solution, the customer had no clue about.

Some believe that they are super salespeople and are capable of selling anything to anybody. Whatever else they may be, they are not professional salespeople as they discard Brian Tracy's Golden Rule.

Others wrongly believe that educating the customer on the technical aspects of the product is primary before selling the product. This is not so. Mattson recommends that 'sell today and educate tomorrow'.

Some fail to remember that the customer is not the only decision-maker. The salesperson, through the finding of needs, also has to come to a decision on what solution is best to satisfy needs.

Glossing over the weakness of a product and hoping the customer will not notice is not a smart strategy. It is better to raise the issue so that the customer can make a studied judgement.

Principles are most necessary to guide the salesperson to an understanding of what is the prerequisite to being a professional.

32

Sales Teams and Unique Contributions

In the high-octane world of modern retail, there are newer ways to get straight to the consumer, by passing all the traditional channels that were, in the past, the cornerstones of sales. There are new dinosaurs in the Jurassic Park of sales.

In consumer products sales, the distributor had been the pivot on which everything swung. The natural network of wholesale distribution which criss-crossed the country pre-dated the onset of the distributor. The distributor was the new kid on the block, a threat to the wholesale network.

Traditional wholesalers worked to handle only popular brands and used low prices as the motive force in pushing products into the village markets. The essential difference between these two channel partners was simple.

The wholesaler sat in the busy by-lanes of the bazaars, and traders came from far and wide to place orders with them. The system was efficient. Most transactions were in cash. The orders placed were packed into cartons and loaded on to trucks that would, in most cases, deliver overnight to the interior markets.

The distributor was different to the wholesaler in that they went in search of the customer. This was done through elaborate mechanisms. They would have a sales team that would carry goods to be sold with a team consisting of the salesperson, driver of the van and the delivery boy. This motley crew would comb the markets and reach products, especially the brands that were not handled by the wholesale network.

At times, the distributor appointed sub-stockists. These were supplied products by the distributor. These stockists did the redistribution within the town they were based. This freed up the distributor to reach more far-flung markets. This many-tiered channel of distribution met a then existing need. Logistics were poor and the banking system archaic. FMCG manufacturers were happy to not have to deal with so many customers. They preferred to deal with a fewer number of distributors who would pay up and stock products.

Procter & Gamble experimented with further reducing the number of distributors, ending up with about 18 for India. These distributors were sizeable companies. The experiment did not work well and they went back to creating more distributors.

Asian Paints was among the first to realize the power of selling direct to a vast number of dealers. They, today, invoice to over 40,000 dealers across the country. They mastered logistics long before others in the industry and became unassailable market leaders. This set the pace for the dropping of channel partners in the quest to serve the consumer better.

Today, Amazon and its ilk have set up an even more formidable chain of supply. It is able, at times, to deliver overnight straight to the consumer.

Anju, an avid reader, saw on Amazon a book she had been looking for but had not been able to find time to shop for. She ordered it online before going to bed. Next morning, she was surprised to find the courier outside her door with the book in hand.

In this churn of times, what is the reason to have a sales team? Would not a fine software do the job? These are the questions that companies have to find answers to. Each salesperson is a challenge to hire, train and hold. Each year, the cost of a salesperson rises. What makes it all worthwhile? What is it that a salesperson can deliver that a sophisticated software cannot?

It will get harder to answer that question with time. Artificial intelligence has amazing options, and boundaries are hard to define. It is clear that sales teams and salespeople are being challenged to provide a unique service that software cannot offer.

It is felt that highly technical products would require face-to-face interaction. Perhaps, the real test would be if sales teams are more productive than a software. Here lies the challenge, doing what is unique and contributing in a manner that makes the process of selling comfortable and more enjoyable for the consumer.

Here is where the concept of relationships in selling comes into play. Transactions can be done with no care to relationship building. Sales while being finite every month-end are also the means of keeping the game of business infinite.

Salespeople must master the skill of selling to the person to help the consumer make a superior choice, not to merely press click on an online catalogue. Consumers need help to decide smarter. Consumers want human interaction and a sense of relationship, beyond the mere transaction.

33

Know What to Pitch

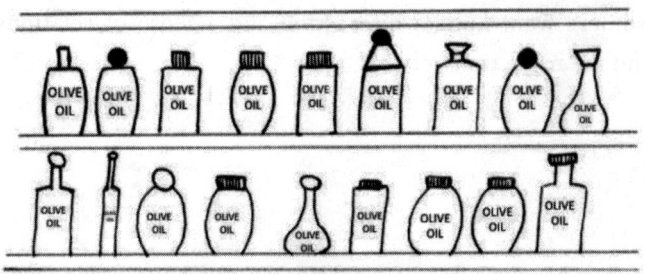

If the presence of the salesperson provides the unique opportunity to interact with the customer, there must be more than just relief that one is not facing an artificially intelligent software. It must, in service and sales terms, account for more. Or, why trouble to create and maintain a sales force?

It is said that benefit statements are the most powerful in bringing in the orders. In sales terms, a benefit is that aspect of the product or service that directly impacts the needs of a customer. In the traditional understanding of selling, there is the school of thought that imagines that the more features and advantages of a product or service are recited during the sales call, the greater the chance of bringing home the bacon.

As a result, there is great emphasis during the induction of a recruit into the sales force to grill down the technical aspects and their advantages over the competitive offering and to consumers at large. Many sales and marketing personnel commit these details to memory. It is a moment of pride as each feature of the solution is presented without error.

In the USA, such selling is rather uncharitably called 'showing up and throwing up'. This is considered the sign of an amateur salesperson, something akin to hitting the customer with book of specifications. Hoping, also that it will leave the customer spell-bound and impressed, it does little to help the customer move closer to the buying decision.

Professor Sheena Iyengar from Columbia Business School had done some interesting work on how choice impacts a customer's buying decision. She reposts that given similar conditions, a reasonable range of choices does help the consumer choose wisely and complete the transaction. However, increase the choice to an extraordinary level and the number of completed buying decisions drops sharply.

Professor Sheena studied two supermarket stores of similar demographics and noted the sales of olive oil. One had a choice of

14 brands. The other had a range of 700 brands. Strangely, the supermarket with the limited range had much more sales of olive oil than the one that stored the massive range of brands.

Her conclusion was that the human brain can work comfortably within a relevant range of product offerings; however, when forced to deal with choice options beyond a reasonable level, rather than cope, the signals get confused and the decision is to delay a buying decision.

This comes into play in every customer's buying situation. When a salesperson barrages a prospect, with an unending list of customer advantages, the mood changes to one of caution, rather than of confidence. It is important that some work be done to classify which advantages have any relevance to the real needs of the customer.

The crucial differentiator is the finding of the 'real needs'. This is what a truly professional salesperson does. She does not prescribe without doing a thorough diagnosis. Medical professionals are not considered to be true unless they follow the rigour of testing and confirming a diagnosis before they take a decision on the treatment to apply.

Salespeople who jump to prescribing the solution without finding out the scope and operating reality of the customer rarely get the sales order. They never get to know why they did not get the order. Perhaps the price was too high! Or was the salesperson just a novice in the selling game?

It is amazing to find how untrained sales teams are in the process of selling. In a review of sales training role-plays, the finding was that over 90 per cent of the sales calls enacted have no regard for what the real needs of the customer are, except to go for the order with gusto. It gets the order to go away from the salesperson.

When a salesperson does not capitalize the advantage of being face to face or directly talking to the prospect, it reduces the crucial differentiator between having a live salesperson and an online shopping software. When this happens, the gates of the modern-day Jurassic Park are flung open. The salesperson who does not understand this is actually risking the future and might have to in time seek career options.

There is little argument that training for a salesperson is beyond just giving an induction programme high on technical knowledge and nothing on the process of selling, relevant to the industry. The dependence on learning on the go, or not ever learning, is too high a price to pay in low productivity and market shares.

34
Breaking Trust

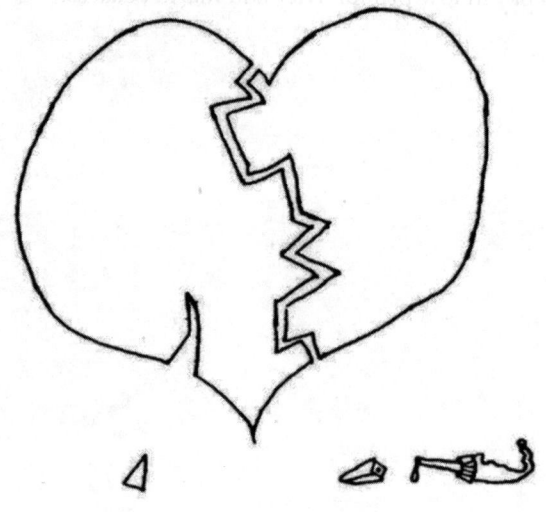

Having established that the overwhelming advantage of having a sales team is the relationships that are built that give salespeople a cutting edge over online catalogue-based selling. The reason for this is the clearer insight into the customer's reality and, more importantly, the real needs, both functional and personal. What is the effect of telling lies on such a delicate relationship?

There was a time, before Fevicol, when an adhesive called 'Quick Fix' ruled the markets. They had an advertising tag line which went like this: Joins everything but broken hearts. Herein is the message. Salespeople who opt to skip the truth to make a momentary brownie point face grave risk on being caught lying.

Ratan was a powerful salesperson and worked hard to make his quotas. He was obsessed with keeping his word to his sales manager. It was the grand closing of sales, the year-end. Ratan was entrusted with bringing in sales orders of $450,000. He felt confident of meeting this commitment as Valzar Industries, his long-standing customer, had been finalizing a mega order.

Ratan had been negotiating with Ramesh Mani, the affable owner chairperson. Their relationship went back strangely to a chance meeting on a railway platform in Erode over eight years ago. They both were waiting to catch a train that was over four hours late. There had been no seat on the platform crowded with passengers awaiting the train. They both sat on their hard case VIP suitcases and struck up a conversation. The train came, they travelled together and parted exchanging visiting cards.

It was Ramesh who took the initiative to keep in touch. Ratan was touched that despite being the proprietor of Valzar Industries, he valued their association. Ramesh invited Ratan to bid for Valzar business. Steadily, the business relationship grew and Ratan was considered a preferred supplier.

This mega deal was one that Ratan worked through the purchase department. As the amount was large, the signing of the order was to be completed by Ramesh himself. At the meeting, Ramesh spoke of his competitor, Balajee Industries, who was trying to break into all Valzar vendors to get a pricing advantage. He asked Ratan if they had approached him. In fact, Ratan had supplied Balajee Industries for the past six months and that account looked promising. Ratan knew that his order was under jeopardy if he admitted that he had in fact supplied Balajee. Ramesh kept looking at Ratan for a response. He shook his head vigorously and denied any contact with Balajee.

Ramesh knew that it was not true. He suddenly got up and said that he had an urgent meeting to attend and left the room to never return. The mega deal fell through. Ramesh never returned calls and Valzar withdrew orders they had placed.

Ratan could never answer the question that kept haunting him for years after, what if he had told the truth?

Relationships thrive on trust. At times, it goes beyond even the realm of business.

R.D. Yadav was an upright salesperson and a pillar of integrity, and the trade took his advice in matters that were even family matters. Once he was asked to intervene between two feuding brothers who had issues about inheritance. Yadav was respected by both brothers. He listened to both and made recommendations that finally solved their dispute.

It went even farther. One of the brothers was matchmaking for his daughter with a prominent businessman of a neighbouring town. Yadav was known to the proposed family. Yadav was requested to join the meeting when the match was discussed and arranged. When the wedding took place, he was given a place of honour at the wedding feast.

Telling the truth and being respected for one's integrity is the added value that brings a negotiation on any business deal to a happy end. The professional salesperson chooses to be forthright and transparent not only because of the moral aspect of the issue but also because it makes good business sense. Those salespeople who understand that theirs is a business of building trust will not take a foolish risk with the lifeline of relationships—trust.

Trust is the most powerful multiplier of sales orders.

35
Dr No

The word 'Yes' has a universal acceptance as a positive one. Lovers seek that as an answer when they 'pop' the question. Children want their parents to give the three-letter response when they ask for anything they want. Friends ask for the same response when they throw a party. Politicians want everyone to say 'Yes' when they ask for votes. How then is the word 'No' such good news to the sales community?

Ian Fleming created the arch enemy for his eternal James Bond, an evil, Dr No. The mere choice of the name has, since 1958, given the word 'No' a rather negative press. It has a certain angry tone to it. One can expect that it will generate some discussion and perhaps some controversy too. 'Yes', on the other hand, has a promise of peace and a certain contentment. How come 'No' is good news to the salesperson?

Perhaps, if there is a single word that has given birth to a profession, it has to be the word 'No'. Imagine the first time a consumer used it to indicate either displeasure or satiation of demand. Perhaps, it was a disagreement about its value and hence an objection to the price. Either way, the 'No' resounded very loud and created worry in the mind of the one selling the goods or service. 'No' can have a ring of finality, not if there is a salesperson close at hand.

The sales profession then can attribute its genesis to the application of the word 'No' to a sale offer. A 'No' uttered by a consumer is never a last word. It, for the salesperson, is the clarion call to arms. That is when the concept of professional selling takes stage. Everything about the nature of selling is an evolved treatise to study the mind of the consumer who says 'No' but means 'Not yet'.

Jack Carew, in his quest for the professional salesperson, came around to the realization that the nature of the assignment is to get the customer to say 'Yes', preferably before he decides to say a 'No, thanks. I am just looking'. Harry J. Friedman, one of the leading minds in modern retailing, wrote a book with just the same title.

Jack felt that his research into sales was best encapsulated in the book he wrote called *You'll Never Get No for an Answer.*

There are processes that go into the decision-making of every consumer. Simon Sinek expounds rather eloquently that all decision-making is in the inner recesses of the brain.

36

The Joy of Professional Selling

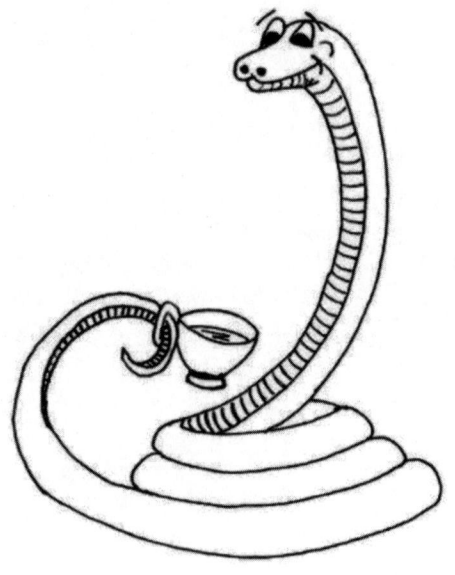

There is something to say about a profession that requires you to be on the road for the better part of the month, travelling to a new market every morning. Motion seems to be the ruling word. One keeps moving, day after day, month after month, and the thread of time whizzes by and suddenly it is all over but the sense of motion does not stop. One feels the motion, but there is no new market to conquer. Little, if any, compares to the joy of a selling job, especially when it is professionally conducted.

There is a vision from a bus as it careens through dusty roads. There are montages of the people one serves; poor and rural, thatched huts and livestock tethered in the small compounds; a continuous rush of green that races by you; and the feeling that this has been happening since ever and that you miss being here. There is retreat from the urban mountains of concrete and the calm that descends as children play with whatever they can, improvising, and squeals of delight no less than Fisher-Price elicits from their well-planned toys.

In train rides, there is another charm. Platforms are interesting fables in the making. Families huddle together and share the simplest of meals, helped down with swigs of what looks unhygienic water. One wonders where all these multitude are setting out to visit.

Sometimes the train stops for no apparent reason, right in the middle of nowhere. There are farms on both side of the track, not a sign of any living creature. Especially after a quick shower of rain, the fields take on an unreal colour and there is an unbearable pull to step down from the train carriage and walk away into a world one left behind and to never return to the life one is living. Maybe, in another lifetime. The strange scene is unfamiliar, comforting and yet inviting, calling to come retrieve what has been lost. Touch the reality of something that is more infinite than the stalking month-end target.

What would life be if one did really step down from the train and never return?

Each town has the look of every other one: a small main street that can be traversed in an easy 15-minute walk, not a toilet in sight and if any is sighted, the stench and mess of the makeshift one makes one long for more reasonable facilities, knowing that there will be no change anytime in the foreseeable future and life will continue to be dusty and dirty. Sewers are always open and clogged, spilling its toxic content that only the unrelenting sun will handle by scorching it clean.

There are few eating places that hungry salespeople flock to like the Ruby Hotel in Jalpaiguri, famed for its fish and thali meal under a creaking ceiling fan. There are only limited places on earth that give more sustenance and succour to those who come seeking it.

There is a little shack in Kolhapur that serves comfort food to those destined to stay away from home—an honest to goodness serving of pure white grained and steaming rice, dunked with a generous dollop of a striking yellow dal, lentils being the staple diet across the markets. Here, hungry salespeople can be seen stuffing huge lumps of rice and giving the look of pure satisfaction. There is bound to be a queue if you land up late.

Outside of Jullundur, there is a favourite highway dhaba that has for its menu only the unbeatable *'Ma de Dal'* and hot tandoori bread. Nothing else is on the menu. A combination to be drowned in a gallon of *chach*, or buttermilk. They churn it in a simple clothes washing machine, as household blenders cannot cope with the demand. One fervently hopes it does not run double shift to do what it was designed for. There is a generosity of spirit. All truck drivers and patrons are welcome to carry away bottles of the chach, making 'one for the road' a truly safe proposition.

The joy of meeting the people is unbeatable. Each day brings a new market, a new customer and a chance to catch up on life that ebbs so rapidly. One of the charms of meeting the trade-up country is their eagerness to spend time with the visitor. A far cry from the perfunctory sales calls afforded in the urban cities. The tea with home-made snacks would be sent from the distributor's kitchen. Lunch would be served by the coy ladies of the household who break up on being complimented for their cooking prowess.

If there is a heaven anywhere, this is it, this is it.

37

Balcony View of Sales

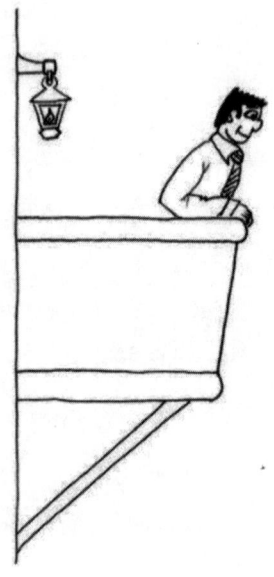

A sale is not complete until the user consumes the product or service. There are other versions of what completes a sale.

'It's not a sale until the paperwork is done', or
'It is not a sale until the money is collected'.

Over the years, there has been emphasis on various aspects of the selling process, to suit the priorities of the day. Today is a wildly shifting scene. The concept of customer satisfaction, which has been so fashionable for over two decades, was more a tribute to a good concept than a serious pursuit. Giving lip service at seminars and industry confederations was sufficient.

With the online burst of activity, the factor of consumer satisfaction has become paramount. All communication is directed at the final consumer. Dates of delivery are predetermined, up to an accuracy of a few hours. Consumers have happily shifted the bar, upwards. Dissatisfaction is much more and vocal. Consumer reviews of product performance are a new area of publicity, with all the pluses and minuses that go with the public declaration of satisfaction.

On looking at sales, the professional view is to ask, what really is the objective of business? This can only be answered if somewhere in all the objects of association, there is a willingness to keep the customer satisfied. Sales as a function cannot have any different goal. Too often salespeople have no understanding or connect with the consumer, who is the user of the product, or service. The only one they meet are their trade customers, be they dealers, stockists or distributors.

As a result, the vision is restricted to the satisfaction of the trade partner. However, this can have little bearing on the satisfaction levels of the consuming person. There are few, if any, instances of paying attention to the real user. It is only when the concern shifts to the user of the product that there will be a free atmosphere to understand the issues that grate at the consumer point.

The concept of 'dumping' is a practice that goes contrary to the concern for the user. Where goods have a 'Use by' date, the chance of getting a good grade from the user will nearly always be difficult. Understanding this potential area of dissatisfaction, sales teams would be conscious of the risk in blocking goods with slow-moving items.

This kind of a balcony view of business is a needed approach if the user is to be kept in focus. This lends itself to a greater appreciation to the process of selling. A robust selling system would take into account all aspects of running a business, over and beyond the making of profits and maximizing shareholder value. When there is such a view, the futility of applying unreasonable pressure is clearly seen as an action which will have jeopardy for the future.

Sales managers are pretty short-sighted as the month-end arrives. Decisions are taken to ensure that some arbitrary estimates or targets for the month are secured. It is a mark of a professional that restraint be applied to ensure that there are no after-effects, post the month's invoicing. Here, the one with the greatest balcony view is the top management. Without their active concern, there would be no real effort to curb this malpractice.

This is an area that is as important as cost control, financial discipline or strategic planning. It needs active management input. It falls into an understanding that professional selling does limit wayward sales behaviour yet has a positive impact on sales numbers. The concern for tertiary movement of goods is still not a popular one, and there are no real measures of how the consumers use the products.

The efforts must be made to keep an eye on how do consumers eye the success of a brand. Social media is a double-edged sword that will work for professional companies and nearly overnight destroy those that do not match up.

38

Evolving into a Sales Professional

What is a professional selling system? How does one know which one to choose? How does it impact the sales team? These and other questions can plague the company seeking to professionalize its sales force. It is not hard to find the answers. This chapter will try to answer these and other questions.

There are certain skills of selling that have to be learnt uniformly by all members of the sales team. A good selling system will spend time introducing the team to both the concepts and the skills that will be used in the interaction with the customer.

Most robust sales systems demand that there be an acceptance of certain sales principles that define the attitude to the customer. In any sales training, there is a need to allot significant time to understand why salespersons do what they do. This is what Simon Sinek refers to as the 'why?' He says that those who work for the pay check end up doing the maintenance level of productivity.

Those who work for a cause give their 'blood, sweat and tears' and can achieve amazing things. So what is the cause that a lowly salesperson can commit to? How about being pledged to making the customer's objectives for success your very own? This is an attitude that is based on a finding that the best results come when the salespersons put themselves in the shoes of the consumer.

This does raise the question that if one commits to the other person's success, who is going to ensure that the company wins? Also, how is that congruent with the 'must sell' targets of the month? The answer to this question truly must come from the top management of the company. How much is the company wedded to the values of selling? If the situation is tough, will the value still hold?

A professional training programme would train to give workable skills to create harmony and build a better relationship. Most sales deals are lost at the point when the customer comes up with an objection. Salespeople panic at this point and either tell lies or lose the order.

The sales process sets out a workable strategy for dealing with objections and if the customer is irate. There are many techniques of not upsetting the customer and yet making the points that are necessary. There have been amazing results to handling objections in this manner. It not only protects the relationship from further damage but also sets the ground for improving on the relationship.

A professional sales training regime will lay out ways to tackle different customer types. This is essential even though the need of the organization is clear and technical; it is important to address the person making the decision. If this person is handled wrong, there is a great likelihood of losing the order.

One very important concept is that of 'First Impression' which needs to be made at the first point of meeting the customer. Many a sale has been aborted at this stage. Thereafter, trying to put things together again is extremely remote. Here is when the company presents its ambassador. Grooming, etiquette and communication skills are part of the package.

A professional selling system is a simple and practical guide to what is expected from the salesperson who is facing the customer for the first or many repeat visits. It lays out step by step the actions that need to be taken to first ascertain the real needs of the customer. This is done through a series of smart questioning techniques.

Having identified the real need, it is also the responsibility of the salesperson to ensure that the customer is made aware of the nature and scope of the need. This sets the stage for an analysis that determines if there is a worthy solution for the needs established. This, too, is a very vital step for it defines the nature of the solution to the problem.

The professional selling system then goes on to prepare for the pitch, when the presentation of the solution is made to the customer. It is necessary to define how the pitch has to be designed and made in a manner that it has impact and wins the order.

Most salespeople dread this moment of truth. The closing is never a sure thing. Using an approved system really helps.

A professional sales system is a prerequisite for working the markets today. Every salesperson facing the customer is money spent in advance. To make it an investment needs an investment in a professional selling system.

Or it is money down the drain.

39
Being in Your Customer's Shoes

There is the old adage that you never understand the other person's issues until you walk a while in her shoes. This is applicable in both life and sales. Sales teams are often so fixed on their own targets and goals that they end up imagining that the customer is an opponent, someone who stands in the way of them attaining their objective.

The moment the customer is considered as an obstacle to their plan achievement, the conditions are being set for a malpractice of sales. Across markets, salespeople tend to be inwardly focused and in their own self-interest. This unfortunately results in poorer sales than those people who can force themselves to be focused on the issues facing the customer.

There is nauseating lip service paid to the customer in all sales literature. The concept of 'Customer is King' has been beaten to death by people who have not the slightest concern for the plight of the customer. Does the success of the customer really figure in a salesperson's priorities? The evidence of so many failed sales relationships do not hold this to be true.

If the customer succeeds, can the salesperson handling the account really fail? This is a question that needs to be realized by the management of sales teams. There are moments of emotion when uncomplimentary and unparliamentary language are used to refer to the trade. Trade making a profit has angered many a sales manager, and there is a tacit belief that this is being done at the expense of the salesperson's target.

Trade has generally been given certain margins for their work and effort in moving goods along the consumer trail. There is always the conflict that while the trade considers the margins inadequate, the salesperson finds that the continued maintaining of their full margin is contra-productive to the movement of sales. They urge that more discounts be given to encourage sales.

Unfortunately, very few salespeople understand the impact of cutting 1 per cent on the distributor's margin. In most consumer products, the margin is as low as 5 per cent at the distributor level.

Dropping a single percentage is tantamount to a 20 per cent drop in margins.

Yet there are other dealers who disturb all price stability by cutting margins relentlessly and contributing to the grey market. Goods that move based on sheer price are, at times, more damaging than a dealer who refuses to cut his margins. However, the former gets all the support from the sales team. In time, the concept of increasing velocity at the cost of the other dealers is a dysfunctional one.

Strangely, the one who survives is the one who stays the course and ensures good market work while upholding the margins.

This concept of 'Who's shoes are you in?' is a major differentiator to the impact companies have in the market place. It appears to be a simple way of looking at the customer. Those who can appreciate such a major concept would go through their career with a huge advantage over those who have no understanding.

In reality, the concern for the success of the customer is the foundation of all relationship building in sales. It helps bring about trust in the start of any relationship. Once there is a condition of trust and rapport, the future of the sales relationship is on firm ground.

This concept also gives scope to consider asking a question, when in doubt, about how to act. Those who practise this technique use a method which allows them to pose a guidance question of 'Is this going to benefit your customer?' This immediately triggers off warning signals that communicate that the transaction is loaded against the customer and needs to be reviewed for prudence.

It becomes a kind of a guiding principle of working the sales circuit. It is also defining the value that the company places on doing business with customers. It is not a mindless commitment to shareholders' value. For sure everybody does business for profit. However, there has to be a way of going there that makes doing business with the company a pleasurable and sustaining one.

Business is an infinite game, as Sinek points out. Companies need to understand that if they wish to play the game.

40

The Salesperson as a Servant

The evolution of selling as recounted in the early part of this book does move on to this age of seeking to satisfy the individual customer, not just a sea of customers. Every customer has a voice today and is a ready platform for every marketing person to plan a campaign for.

Dr Ranjit Nair, CEO of Germin8, a Mumbai-based company that has a means of culling the views of customers to understand what they are saying about specific brands across the various social media platforms, has this to say about the new voice of the single consumer.

> Consumers today are empowered because they are able to express themselves on social media sites like Facebook and Twitter, where they discuss their needs, opinions and experiences with brands. Many of these conversations are public in nature and are rich in terms of the consumer insights they contain.
>
> Analytics companies like Germin8 allow brands to tap into these social media conversations to understand their consumer better, improve the services they offer their customers and also improve how they communicate with them. Germin8 does this by trawling the web for consumer conversations in real time, and then mining these conversations for insights using Artificial Intelligence algorithms.

Social media is replete with examples of how salespeople have deliberately lied to consumers just to make a sale. For instance, according to Dr Nair, one of the leading contributors of negative sentiment about brands is consumers complaining about mis-selling by salespeople, especially in sectors like life insurance which are difficult for a layperson to understand. The short-term benefit of making these sales is much less than the damage caused by losing the relationship with the customer and the long-term damage to the brand's reputation.

The power of the early salesperson came from the knowledge that was the clear domain of the seller. The consumer succumbed to the array of information bytes that was shot at her. Today, the monopoly of information is available to anyone willing to type 'Google' into any smartphone. The roles have to change.

Sharon Drew Morgen in her work *Selling with Integrity* speaks of the need to reinvent sales by reengineering the salesperson.

Morgen has this to say: 'In the nicest ways, with the nicest people, with the highest principles in mind, sales has promoted disrespect.... Sales, the preeminent business skill, has assumed the ultimate insult: to serve itself'. No harm in that, except in doing so, reduces the worth and, in the short-term too, the productivity of sales.

The need is to serve the customer and not necessarily the product one is selling. The expertise that the salesperson brings to the party is the ability to understand the prospect's situation in totality, from the questioning and information sought, to be able to get the consumer to realize the needs as applicable. At the end of the exercise, there may be no sale of the product one is pushing, if the solution so warrants it. This is serving the consumer and will over a period of time pave the way to greater sales productivity.

The shift is from selling to buying. Previously, salespeople were meant to sell (at any cost!) the product, with the motto 'Buyer beware'; today, the difference is that the salesperson facilitates the consumer in the buying decision. So the consumer is not being sold the product but helped to buy it.

Sharon adds rather emphatically,

> And since people only buy what they need, the way they need it, from people they trust, it doesn't matter how useful or powerful or wonderful my product is if people don't trust that I have their best interests at heart. Ultimately, all I have is me and my ability to serve.

Doing this in no way reduces sales orders. It, in fact, has a positive effect on the sales environment and there is a dramatic increase in sales, there is joy abounding, both with the customer and the selling person. This is the new age of selling. An age that values respect, collaboration and a will to make each day count in service.

41

Handling Objection
and Irate Customers

Handling a 'No' is a part of every salesperson's daily routine.

Each salesperson develops a home-grown style and blunders forward. It is unfortunate that worldwide, the single greatest loss of sales is attributed to inept handling of objections by the salesperson. Here is a major point of sales order leak. A professional sales programme can easily define an objection-handling system that can plug this loss of productivity.

There are various ways that are suggested to handle this situation in a professional manner. *Forbes* has a seven-step method.

There are many behavioural tips on how to handle it. The most relevant one is to remain calm. This is easy to prescribe but often hard to implement. When someone is shouting at you and is near abusive, it takes a lot to remain cool. However, this can be self-taught and practised. This creates a detached involvement.

Another good tip is to tell yourself that this is not about you, even if you own the company. It is about a situation, possibly where you were not involved. Yet the customer sees you as an ambassador of the company and she wants redress, or at least a patient and caring hearing.

The general advice is to listen and do what is called 'active listening'. This is an activity that is apparently passive but really a calculated effort to understand the customer's point of view objectively. This could be done by taking down bullet point notes.

The next step is to ensure that there is sympathy for the customer's story, rather than a judgemental attitude which the customer can pick up quickly. This could cause the interaction to go south and create loss.

The next step is to gracefully apologize, if there is cause for one. Often salespeople feel that an apology is incriminating and should be avoided. There is also another ploy used called the 'pre-emptive apology'. This is when the apology is rendered without just cause. This can be poorly taken if used without sensitivity.

Having done all the five other steps, it is time to search for a reasonable solution. This could be a full solution or even some guidelines on where to find the solution. This is the most important part of the interaction.

There are additional tips for smoothening out the possible chinks in the line-up.

There are those that feel that using the customer's name in the course of the conversation brings in a certain closeness, which helps build rapport. This has cultural limitations. There are places where familiarity can be misunderstood for a certain cockiness, which is not needed here.

There is another technique that forces one to be friendly and more likeable. This is to smile while talking to the angry customer. Although this might appear fake, there is a discipline it forces. You can't be speaking rude if there is a big smile on the face.

Sometimes it helps to press the mute button on the phone, especially if the customer is getting out of hand. It will block the inadvertent acknowledgements that might communicate any cynicism.

This appears to be a simple and straightforward method but it has deeper connotations.

As one listens to an objection, it is a gateway to understanding what is going on in the mind of the customer. At times, the customer only speaks part of what is on his mind. This exercise is to listen to understand the reality of the customer's objection. Why is it so important to him?

Acknowledging is as simple as a nod of the head, good eye contact or quick verbal sound to show that what is being said is well received. It allows for time to assess what is being said and has a tranquilizing effect on the customer who recognizes a friend in the time of need.

Having heard the objection, the vital step is to uncover the 'why?' of the objections. It gives valuable feedback as to the state of the customer's mind. If there is a way to tilt the objection to a 'yes, maybe…', this is the moment. Once all the relevant data is received, the scene is set to deal with the objection.

The process allows for the best way to deal with a customer's objection. It also allows for closer bonding with the customer. This is the time when the solution to the customer's objection can be laid out, hopefully drawing one closer to getting the order.

42

Always Diagnose
Before You Prescribe

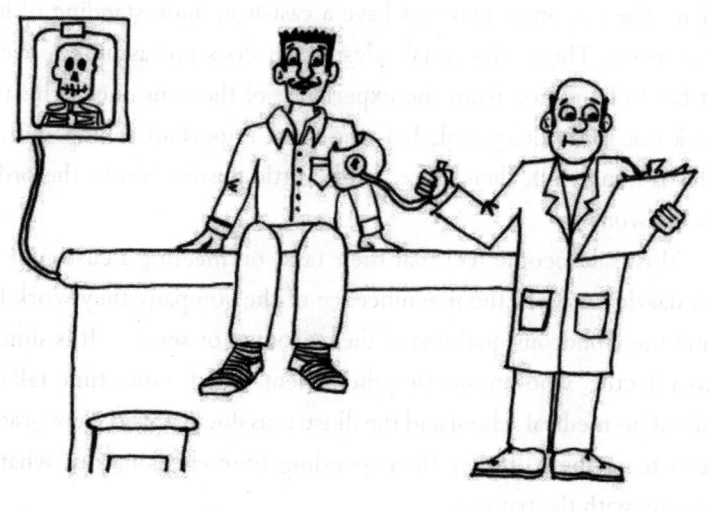

One of the most important skills that a professional salesperson must have is the ability to identify the need of the customer.

No one ever bought anything unless they needed it. Think about it. However ridiculous the purchase and even if there was no imaginable utility, a purchase feeds an apparent or potent need. The need may be just momentary and not last. However, for the moment that it was present and relevant to the buyer, there was a need being fulfilled.

Salespeople often wonder why the order slipped away. Most often it is attributed to an unfavourable price. The truth could be far from that. The customer may not have a cast-iron understanding of her real need. The professional salesperson does not assume a need. It has to be mined from the experience of the consumer. This is a task not to be delegated. It is the most important selling skill. If this is done well, then there will be little obstruction to the order being won.

Most salespeople feel that their task, on meeting a customer, is to dazzle her with the magnificence of the company they work for and the wondrous qualities of their product or service. It is similar to a doctor, who on meeting the patient spends more time talking about his medical school and the illustrious doctors who were graduates from there, rather than spending time checking out what is wrong with the patient.

It is the task of every salesperson to understand where the customer currently is and in how many ways she is unhappy with the experience of using the product. If these ways can be identified and the customer realizes the nature of these gaps, it is the start of the possibility of a sale. No gap, no sale.

So how does one go about professionally defining the need?

There are four questions that work well for an exploratory session. These are as follows:

1. Mood questions: These are questions intended to open up the prospect to share as much about the industry and company working.
2. Diagnostic questions: These are meant to start analysing the current satisfaction levels with the product being used and to determine where the dissatisfactions are.
3. Got it! questions: On discovering the possible needs of the customer, or the gap, it is now important that the customer realize the importance of doing something to satisfy the need. Only if this is acknowledged by the customer will she make an effort to fulfil it.
4. Going forward questions: These are questions that ask for an opportunity to present a solution to the realized needs.

A professional selling system will also define the first contact with the prospect. This is crucial to the success of the visit. There is need to have a favourable impression at first contact, every time the salesperson calls on a prospect. The energy, the attitude and the appearance of the sales team are important factors that open up a selling opportunity.

This drill of identifying and getting the customer to realize the gap or need is the single most important contribution that a salesperson can make. This differentiates the everyday salesperson from the professional one. The more sharply a salesperson identifies the needs, the greater the chance that the final order will favour the professional.

Yet in a survey conducted by B-More Consulting, among the salespeople attending sales programmes, 95 per cent do not work to identify needs. At best, they only address the technical or functional needs. No one ever bothers to track the personal needs of the decision-makers. When after the programme they try out the new techniques, there is a substantial improvement in sales closing ratios.

It pays to diagnose before prescribing solutions. A professional salesperson will do it no other way.

43
Meeting the Purchaser's Needs

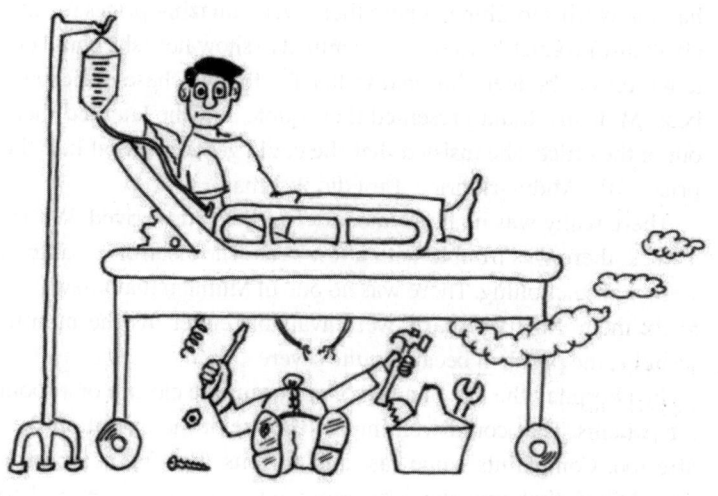

One of the realizations that sales professionals have to deal with is the varied types of customers that they have to interact with. While everything could be right with the product offering, there may still be a 'No' at the time of asking for the order. It may have nothing to do with the product, or service, but everything to do with the salesperson.

It was a brand new hospital in Mumbai and the newly appointed purchase head Tara had a bee in her bonnet. She in her previous job had many trips to China, where there were amazing prices for just about any product. Tara was determined to show how she could cut down on the budget allocated to her for the purchase of hospital beds. Midmark India presented their quote and she laughed them out of the office. She insisted that she could get the beds at half the price of the Midmark price. Tara did just that.

There really was no honeymoon when the beds arrived. Within a week, there was trouble with a few beds. The electronic controls were malfunctioning. There was no one in Mumbai that knew how to fix them. No spare parts were available either. As the months went by, the problem became quite severe.

In a hospital, the loss of a bed often means the closure of a room for patients. That could well impact the use of the operation theatre too. Complaints came fast and furious. The finance person complained that revenue was being hit. The nurses refused to handle the beds and, finally, the owner took a bold decision to scrap the beds and buy local.

Tara had been the target of all the complaints and she rued the day she had not bought the Midmark ones as they were manufactured just a little away from Mumbai, in Umbergaon. She asked Midmark to present their offer again. This time Tara had no hesitation in placing the whole order with Midmark.

In the space of the better part of the year, Tara had totally reversed her personal needs when it came to buying hospital beds.

This is the reason that salespeople must try and ask themselves what is it that the buyer needs, apart from the functions of the product.

It is also possible that the needs can change over time, especially if anything serious happens in the interim. The professional salesperson is trained to both explore the functional needs of the customer and to assess what is critical to the decision-maker.

As the centre of a sales team's working is the concept of relationship building; this ability to identify what makes the purchaser want to buy is a crucial differentiator. While there are many ways to categorize the types of customers and also varied strategies to best handle them, it is not really necessary to be able to slot each customer into any special cubicle.

It is more important to train the salesperson to not assume. This is more rampant with the older and experienced salespeople. They are more likely to fall into the profiling trap. The car you drive, the watch you wear, the smartphone brand, all tell tales. Sometimes they can be misleading.

The safest way is to go through the process of finding out. Being diligent about it makes the way surer. Responding to each need identified is more important than pigeonholing for comfort. This also handles the aspect of salesperson getting jaded on the job. It is also important to periodically review the personal needs of those that have had long associations. There is the danger of getting over familiar and being taken for granted.

There is an old truth that has stood the test of time. People buy from people they like, all other criteria being nearly same. Are the right people being hired to face the customers? Or is the battle being lost just at the very start? Ambassadors of the company must project the company, both in its values and in the shallow aspects of personality and grooming.

The sales team is a significant cost factor. It is a pity that they are not optimized. This is avoidable damage.

44

Sales Functional Needs
and Personal Aspirations

The focus of every professional salesperson is to get to the gap, or needs, as quick as possible. It is this that triggers out the possible solution. If inept work has been done on the realizing of needs, there will be a weak stance with the customer, with prayers and divine enticements being offered to appease the gods that worry about such matters.

Having rechecked the need, it is now important to fall back on the technical sessions to bring a fit between the needs of the customer and the advantages of the product or service. The salesperson should be trained to capture these moments. One of the standard exercises could be on the FABs, also known as features, advantages and benefits.

Most salespeople see no difference between these three words. They consider them to be interchangeable in use. The common logic is that if one can spout advantages of a product, more is better. Many just learn by rote and hope to impress by just disgorging information on the customer. Herein lies the difference between a trained professional salesperson and a hustler.

The concept of FABs clearly separates the men from the boys.

A feature is just a tangible aspect of the product that is part of what makes up the total package. It is also true that there has to be a use or an advantage to every feature present in the product. In fact, there cannot be a feature without at least one advantage. It is possible that a product has 10 discernible features. These 10 features could have 10 or more advantages. Sometimes the advantages could add up to be many times the number of features.

While an impressive array of features can positively impact the buying decision, remember the findings of Dr Sheena Iyengar, where choice beyond a workable number is dysfunctional to the buying decision. Imagine how much more confusing it could be when the advantages parroted out by the salesperson has little relevance to the real need of the consumer. It then is truly contraproductive to selling.

The use of the word 'benefit' is immersed in the word 'advantage'. The average salesperson is only aware of the value of telling the customer the advantages of the product. He believes that in doing so, he is giving the customer the benefits. There is a huge difference between the two words.

An advantage is a mere communication of the advantages of the many features, without any concern for the real needs of the customer. Only when a need is identified by the salesperson and the particular need can be met by one of the features of the product being sold is there a benefit. Put rather simply, a benefit is an advantage of a feature that wholly or partly meets the needs of the customer.

A benefit, therefore, is a feature of the product that is perfect for the need. An advantage without the need of a customer is not a benefit. It is said that only professional salespeople make 'benefit statement' to their prospects. Amateurs just 'show up and throw up'. A customer who is being sold based on specifically the gap or the need is focused on the need satisfaction and will move towards closing the order.

There is often a debate about what harm is there if all advantages are told to the customer. It is argued that it could still impress the customer, even if the advantages are not relevant to that particular customer. Professional selling is about being sure and not vague. Salespeople must believe that the process they are adopting works for the winning of the sale. This will give them the confidence that makes them more persuasive in the sales interaction.

The purpose of a clear-cut selling system is to ensure that the salesperson applies the mind and stays on track, so that the order is won.

45

Pitching It for Impact

When a salesperson gets up to make a pitch before a prospect, it is show time. This is the most important stage of the selling process. Everyone in this situation is bound to have the doubts. Most who stand up to deliver are praying hard that all goes well and that the customer is in a generous mood. It does not have to be so. It is possible not only to calm those fears with proper training but also to be certain that the presentation hits the bullseye, every time.

While nothing beats practising hard, a badly constructed presentation will remain just that—bad. There are an amazing number of experts who offer to solve all presentation problems in a five-minute YouTube video. This seems strange as speaking before an audience is considered the single most common phobia across the world. More people would run rather than present.

There are certain universal truths about designing a presentation. In the early 1970s, all advertising media planners spoke of the need to have an 'Opportunity to See' (OTS) of three. This meant that any advertising message, to be remembered, had to be seen three times by a customer in all media out together.

Later on, another thumb rule was established called the rule of three. The rule was to 'tell them', three times.

The first rule is:	Tell them what you plan to tell them. (Intro)
The second rule is:	Tell them what you came to tell them. (Message)
The third rule is:	Tell them what you had told them. (Summary)

From these indications of presenting for impact, the visual rule of designing a balanced presentation is to consider it as a human body. The head is for the introduction as the audience is told what the topic is about. The chest and body above the legs stand for the subject matter of the presentation. The legs are a summary of what had been presented.

These unchanging rules of presenting for impact are also part of any self-respecting sales system. This is a simple step-by-step method of professional pitching.

As soon as the customer is in the right frame of mind to listen, it is important that the needs as identified earlier are restated to bring the focus to the solution which is to be presented.

On being permitted to present the solution to the customer's needs, the pitch goes to the heart of the matter. In measured terms, the benefits statements are made to fully address only the real needs of the customer. At the point of developing the aspects of the solution, there may be objections that could be raised by the customer. These could easily be handled by using any system of objection handling.

One of the lesser known techniques for greater effectiveness is the concept of checking with the customer if the presentation is relevant to her each time there is a point of order being made. Using a professional presentation template is the best insurance for success, provided, of course, the needs have been correctly assessed.

With such clear directions for a pitch, the salesperson steps up with confidence and the knowledge that he is well prepared and skilful to handle any eventuality. This is the reason why there is no need to fear. As one keeps using a particular presentation system, the confidence grows. People buy from those who present confidently.

It is said that among the fundamental rights there is a need to include a right to be right. This is what Jeff Bezos spoke of at a seminar. When asked what trait he would look for in a potential employee, he said that he would look for an employee who was 'right' more times than wrong. In other words, successful people are valuable in any enterprise.

To be successful is the best multiplier of performance. Each time one succeeds, there is motivation to try for another win. It is necessary that each person has the sweet taste of success. Before this seems outlandishly optimistic, it is worth mentioning the context of the word 'success'.

Each person has a special potential. As this potential is actualized, the bells of success ring loud and clear. The sound of the bell reverberates through the person, resetting hopes for another win.

Winners have no need to lie.

46

The Professional Salesperson

Each day one is exposed to the difficulty of being a professional. It was an internal flight by one of the most extensively flown airlines. Seated on the row no. 10 was a typical sales manager trying to get in a message before the aircraft was closed for a flight.

A burly young man, the sales manager, was talking loudly into the smartphone, unable to hold the decibel down. 'Listen', he badgered,

> We did 15 truckloads last month and I want you to hold that level. No way am I going to accept that we drop down to 10 truckloads. I don't care what you need to do. Keep it at 15, at any cost. Or I will not be able to save you.

It appears that when sales strategy is not effective, a high decibel round of haranguing is the next best alternative.

Sales managers are, unfortunately, not professional themselves. Imagine the state of the junior who received such a phone call. What are the choices? Not a single suggestion was made on how to raise the number of truckloads to more than 10, except a call to arms with a toothless strategy. If there is any situation where lies and bluster are called for, this is one!

Imagine the same situation with a professional sales manager. What would be the difference? For a start, it would be to visit the planned strategy and review the progress on all the action points that were made to have produced the required 15 truckloads. After examining the potential order prospects, there could be a review of any extraordinary possibilities of new customers.

At the end of the review, the professional sales manager would say,

> Please make every effort to complete the action points as we had planned. Do not do anything to jeopardize the relationships you have built. Check with your customers about the way forward and let us get back to review if our strategy is in need of any modification.

There is a morning after. It has to be understood that professionals play the infinite game; each month is just a milestone in the ongoing game of business. You win some, you lose some. You never lose all the time or win all the time, not if you understand that sales is a process and it has little ability to address all the unpredictable variables that strike in a finite sales month-closing. Every new variable that negates a current strategy can be handled, if calm and serious thought is applied to the available information. One has to keep the game going, according to Sinek.

There is a need that everyone, in any profession, can go to sleep each night, knowing that though all the problems of the world are not solved, what was expected of the individual was completed. Some of the actions produced satisfactory results, while others could have been better. The ability of going to sleep should be a factor of having done the job that was expected of the person. The results of course matter. In the long run, a single month has limited impact.

It is interesting to listen to people who have recently retired. As they speak of their career, the highlights of achievements definitely are a source of comfort. The low moments blur in memory. The high of a single month or the depth of depression of a bad month never figures. Life and business are infinite games.

As complicated software brings in refined information, one is led to believe that increasingly business will get more logical and predictable. Unfortunately, it is subject to more knee-jerk strategy than ever before. Every time a planned strategy is upset by seemingly valuable tactics, the impact is dissipated and the strategy lies by the wayside. Sales managers are wont to ask, 'Am I to deliver on a strategy or the result?'

Herein lie some points to ponder.

What is the role of senior sales management? Is it to meet the targets or to create the conditions for meeting the target? Too often, there is this urge to intervene and take matters into hand. This is justified under the duress of the commitment of the month. One has to meet the numbers at all cost. What does this do to all the process?

The salesperson feels inadequate. The intervention of the boss to achieve the numbers is an extraordinary activity, not part of the salesperson's normal arsenal. The salesperson loses face, confidence and worth. However, the sales were gained. At what cost was it gained? What was the abiding loss to the system?

Therein is the need to ponder.

47

Develop Your Team

As one looks at the problem of professionalizing the sales force, the weakness appears to be the bosses. Training the team is the prime responsibility of each sales manager who leads a team. Yet this is where the gap is.

In a recent review of sales managers, among all surveyed, only 7 per cent considered the development of those reporting to them as one of their main responsibilities. Sadly, sales managers see the beating of targets as the only object. Very few see their job as facilitating their teams in meeting targets.

It is interesting to see a salesperson visit a customer with his boss. Invariably, the meeting is conducted by the senior person. The salesperson in charge of the customer just makes the appropriate introductory noises and allows the boss to hold court. There is no one observing how the salesperson deals with his customer or a review of the call, from the perspective of the front-line salesperson.

In another review of what development activity sales managers adopt, there was an overwhelming number (85 per cent) who said that they were developing their people. When asked to show some evidence of their efforts, there was a confused look. 'Of course, we develop our team. We just don't jot it down'. When their teams were quizzed about the developmental inputs given to them by their sales managers, about 8 per cent spoke of having been coached by their boss. So is there anything really happening?

Many companies invite external faculty to bring in professional training and to develop their teams. While this is a good start, real and ongoing training can be done only by the sales managers. Not everyone is comfortable to stand and deliver in front of a class; however, the real training for sales teams is in the market. Every sales manager has to understand the role of fully equipping the front line to handle all customers, big or small.

There are sales heads who are comfortable telling everyone that their team is under par. The implication is that only with the personal efforts of the sales managers the sales numbers are being met. It is a pity that admitting the inadequacy of the team is, in itself, a declaration of the poor capability of the sales managers. Yet, they are blissfully unaware of their area of improvement.

It is time that the supervisory levels of the sales management team understand that while they are committed to making the sales goals of the company, their role is to make it happen through the individual members of the sales team. Every individual on the team is a singular responsibility.

Often sales managers compensate for the weak links of the team with higher performance from the more capable. While this may help meet the month's quotas, it is raising two problems. The first is the need to get the salesperson who is underperforming to grow into an area of competence. The second is the strain on the territory that is overperforming on its targets.

Overperforming on targets is a sign of either underestimating potential of the territory or undue pressure being applied. This could in time boomerang and create a fissure in an otherwise perfectly tended market. Unfortunately, the madness of the month-end overwhelms every other consideration. Here too, the issue is worth considering, how professional are sales managers?

There is a lot been written of how poorly salespeople in the front line are trained. This does not improve as one goes up the sales pyramid. Who really teaches a hotshot salesperson on promotion how to be the complete boss? Most up the rankers, who find themselves in jobs they got promoted to, are unclear about what constitutes their new responsibility, except for the sudden rush of paperwork and administration responsibilities.

With a few weeks of their new assignment, they catch themselves longing for their old position. Life was simpler then. They knew what to do and did not have to endure the clumsy efforts of their poorly trained team. They find that intervening and doing their junior's task themselves brings better sales results than hoping for an improved sales from the underperforming members of the team.

This perpetuates a cycle of sales inadequacy, both for the one in the front line who does not know how to cope and for the increasingly overworked and irritable sales manager who finds the pressure from upper management and the sales team unbearable. The scene is set for more fear and worry.

48

Creating a Resident Faculty

The greatest multiplier of sales performance is the development of the sales team. This is not highly appreciated or understood. Sales teams hanker for discounts and sales promotions, hoping that sales will multiply. Practically, these efforts are at most times contra-productive.

The high of a sales month with a sales promotion is to be considered with the drooping sales of the post-sales promotion months. If not well designed, the months following the sales promo end up negating the wins of the campaign. Along with it, other parameters of stability are hurt such as accounts receivable and credit notes post the end of the programme.

Development of the sales team is not a gain that dips with time. Improved sales abilities and disciplined working ensures that whatever the market turns, the juggernaut of a well-trained team will get the maximum results from the market. This explains how, in downturns of the economy, established brands improve their market shares even if their absolute volumes are not reflecting any gain.

There is no doubt that investments in sales team development have the best returns among all inputs to improve sales. It also need not be very expensive.

Every company, regardless of their size, can afford it. The idea is to create a group of competent high-potential individuals who have reasonable communication skills. They must be formed into a resident faculty of the company. It is important that this team report to the head of sales. There are two reasons for this.

The first is to demonstrate that the issue of developing the team has the highest priority. The whole team will understand that this activity has top-management backing. The more important is the opportunity for the faculty, who are the high potential of the sales team, who work in close proximity to the sales chief and who develop their own understanding of the tasks that move a sales team to success.

This was done very successfully in a company under siege. After the Bhopal tragedy, the atmosphere in the company that was involved in it, Union Carbide, was very turbulent. The employees were shell shocked and suffered from a guilt by association. The Eveready Battery division was the mainstay of the company, and it was critical that people stay motivated and not quit. There were many efforts made to keep communication within the company active. However, the gloom was perceptible. The future was uncertain.

The managing director, Mr V.P. Gokhale, took a decision to invest in training as a visible means to communicate to all employees that there is a future. He constituted the largest ever training initiative in the history of the company. It was mandatory for each employee to attend an eight-hour classroom training programme called, without much fuss, Basic Training Program (BTP).

He insisted on a couple of principles. First, no training module would, in any way, attempt to orient the employees to a 'management point of view'. Quite simply put, no brainwashing. The second was that workers be referred to as junior-most employees. This was to dissolve the 'we–they' divide that is so much a part of the industrial relations code. There were over 6,000 employees to be covered in over 28 locations across India.

To get this done in record time, 44 high-potential staff from all locations were chosen to attend a five-day, train-the-trainer programme at the Airport Hotel in Calcutta. Over the five days, there was a sea change among the participants when they were made to face the challenge before them.

Each of the trainers were asked to translate the modules and be ready to hold the eight-hour programmes in their locations. Despite fears of union opposition, there was a tremendous reception to this unique initiative. BTP was the turning point of the company's transformation into a lean organization and steadily raised the bar in quality and productivity. The gains for the faculty were noteworthy.

Of the 44 strong faculty, called lovingly the BTP gang, 62 per cent were promoted in a period of 18 months. 84 per cent of them were promoted in four years. They continued to take leadership roles in the company and had an attitude of 'Big Brother' to all their teams.

Building a resident faculty is a really worthwhile effort. It builds sales.

49
Too Proud to Lie

This book started with asking the question, why do many salespeople have such a reputation for being shy of the truth? It is no doubt true that there are sales heroes who do not stoop to conquer. The better question is, why, at all, is there a need to resort to such tactics.

It appeared that one of the grave gaps in sales is the functioning of a robust sales system. More so, there is a lack of understanding about what is good selling and what connotes poor selling attitudes. This is where there needs to be clarity among the sales leaders about what is expected of their team.

It is necessary for the leaders to define their beliefs. These are specific to what is considered good selling and to holding on to it even as times grow tough. Leadership is about being a role model during a storm, not just in blue lagoon waters. It is also required that the activities expected from the team be listed so that every member of the sales team is clear what their role is in bringing home the bacon. Results have to be assessed, not merely against budgets but also for what aspects of the sales strategy are effective or need to be modified.

The benefit of doing this is to free the salesperson from avoidable and unnecessary worry. When this happens, the joy of selling is refreshed. Amazing things happen when a sales team is engaged in their work and are on a roll. They actually are capable of wondrous results, which is why it is said that the single largest multiplier of sales performance is a well-developed sales team.

> Sudhakar was a timid salesperson whose inadequacy on the targets was more than made up by his pleasing personality. He could be trusted to do everything that was required of a sales executive dealing with distributors of South Maharashtra. It was a routine sales meet for the trade, and the branch manager called Sudhakar and told him that he being a Marathi could offer a vote of thanks at the end of the programme.

Sudhakar went into a freeze. He had never spoken to a group. He was shy even without having to speak in public. He thought about the impending embarrassment. On the day of the sales meet, he requested permission to speak in English, though his mother tongue was Marathi. He felt more official in English, and more confident. When his turn came, he had written out the vote of thanks and managed to do a fair job of it between sips of water and bouts of stammering.

Sudhakar was very pleased with the experience. He went back to the branch manager and requested that at the next meet, he be allowed to handle a full session. He grew in confidence, and interestingly, his sales grew too. He became one of the highest contributors to the growth of the Maharashtra branch. It is true. An engaged salesperson doesn't dread sales. Sudhakar had found his 'Why?'

Why do I do what I do?

Developing a sales member to be on top of the job is the single most important and unique contribution any sales manager can make. If that is not done, there is no one in the organization that will step in to fill in and develop the individual. This is why schoolteachers that are remembered decades later by their pupils are those that helped develop them as children.

Imagine having a sales team in which every member is a master of the sales system, with superior sales skills. Something like having a Navy SEALs team working for you. Each SEAL is a proud product of the most severe survival training known to humankind. Yet a Navy SEAL is never born, always churned and honed to the perfection possible. How is it that sales teams are supposed to do their own training?

Among the SEALs, there is nothing greater than the team's honour and its survival. It is said that SEAL training is such that each SEAL has to be guarding and protecting their teammates around them. It is their code for success. It does not come instinctively. It is embedded as a prerequisite for being a SEAL. What are the requirements to be a sales team member?

Would a SEAL ever lie? They are taught to be proud of what they are. They are trained to be fearless. A SEAL would be too proud to lie.

Epilogue

The salesperson is the hero of this book. Salespeople, despite all their perceived shortcomings, are a tribe that needs to be honoured and treasured. They are a special people, who live their lives with all their heart. They are ready to go the extra mile and support their friends and even those they have never met before. They have generosity in their heart.

The profession is physically very demanding.

Rohan, who was introduced in an earlier part of this book, shared an experience. He was sent to Solapur as a substitute for a vacationing salesperson. Within days, he contracted a virus and was suffering from cold, cough and severe dysentery. Yet he dragged himself to the market. Finally, he had to be taken to the train station and placed in a compartment.

On reaching Bombay, he was asked to immediately leave for Dhule, one of the most backward districts in Maharashtra. He was certain that in his condition, he would be in a grave situation. Yet he would not call the branch manager and plead for rest. He decided, instead, to make the trip a fun one.

Water is the main source of all free-flowing bacteria. In those days, no bottled or mineral water was available. To protect his stomach from a further attack, he carefully used an electric hob and boiled the water he would drink. Having a stove in his hotel room, he got adventurous and started cooking simple meals each night. Rohan had the happiest memory of his Dhule challenge and to this day speaks fondly of the experience.

The sales community is full of charming personalities, and when two or more gather, it is definitely a happy time. Friendships are formed that last a lifetime. As relationship building is their forte, they forge lasting relationships. There is also a bonding between the trade and the salespeople, which outlasts even the business ties.

Imagine the new salesperson, one who has been formally inducted into a rigour of a rational sales system. The new salesperson is committed to doing good by his customer. He will refuse to sell more to a customer, if that action could stray into the realm of sales malpractice. In doing so, the customer is best served and, truly, so too is the company the salesperson represents. A sale that is not consummated by the final user is not a complete sale.

Each entrant into the sales team requires a twofold development.

The first to be taught are the skills of any professional selling programme. This will drive away doubts of self-worth, similar to anyone else who sets out to be a professional. The second part of the sales development is to adopt a selling process or a sales system. It will force the acknowledgement of the need for an accepted sales process. As the skill is practised in the field, a sense of conscious competence will get embedded.

Winning or losing can never be guaranteed. It is the application of the process of professional selling that needs to be assured. The message is clear. When in doubt, apply the selling process. The results will follow.

This kind of confidence in the sales system is what makes telling the truth so much more comfortable. When the truth is a guiding force, the mind is at ease.

Salespeople are winners. They have no need to lie.

About the Author

Roshan L. Joseph is a professional in the sales and marketing field and a consultant of repute. He has been the Executive Director on the Board of Eveready Industries India Ltd with the accountability for marketing and sales and the Managing Director (MD) of Franke, a Swiss MNC in the kitchen solutions business. At Eveready, he was instrumental in bringing Eveready out of the cold with the path-breaking advertising campaign 'Give Me Red'. This brought about the repositioning of Eveready as a brand that could connect with the youth. The campaign won 11 advertising and marketing awards and continues to date, with the way Eveready advertises. Earlier on, his skills as a marketer were put to test in a challenge facing the flashlight business. This was the neglected business of the company. Today, with adept marketing moves, it is a very profitable division of the company.

In 2004, Roshan, as the MD of Franke, had the challenge of establishing the brand, though no. 1 worldwide, in the Indian kitchen scene. Today, Franke is well established as a premium brand of kitchen sinks. Here too, he established a unique positioning and developed distribution to develop the brand.

In 2007, he started a marketing and sales development company of his own in collaboration with Carew International of Cincinnati, USA. He has worked with diverse clients across the Middle East and India. Roshan has been a trainer as far back as he can remember. He has been the Course Director of the Calcutta Management Association for a record six years. He established the first Sales Training Department in the company. He was the Founder of the Eveready Academy of Sales Training (EAST) and was instrumental in the award-winning initiative Basic Training Program (BTP) for training all employees of Union Carbide, over 6,000 of them.

Roshan is currently the Managing Partner of B-More Consulting (www.bmoreconsulting.net), where he promotes various international sales development initiatives.